STEP-BY-STEP
bread

STEP-BY-STEP
bread

Caroline Bretherton

LONDON, NEW YORK,
MUNICH, MELBOURNE, DELHI

Editorial Assistant David Fentiman
Senior Editor Alastair Laing
Project Art Editor Kathryn Wilding
Senior Art Editor Sara Robin
US Editor Rebecca Warren
Managing Editor Dawn Henderson
Managing Art Editor Christine Keilty
Senior Jacket Creative Nicola Powling
Production Editor Siu Chan
Production Controller Claire Pearson
Creative Technical Support Sonia Charbonnier
Photographers Howard Shooter, Michael Hart

DK INDIA
Assistant Editor Ekta Sharma
Designer Divya PR
Managing Editor Glenda Fernandes
Managing Art Editor Navidita Thapa
DTP Manager Sunil Sharma
DTP Operator Rajdeep Singh

First American Edition, 2012

Published in the United States by
DK Publishing
375 Hudson Street
New York, New York 10014

11 12 13   10 9 8 7 6 5 4 3 2 1

001–180674–May/2012

Copyright © 2012 Dorling Kindersley Limited

Published in Great Britain by Dorling Kindersley Limited.

A catalog record for this book is available from the
Library of Congress.

US ISBN 978-0-7566-9266-7

DK books are available at special discounts when
purchased in bulk for sales promotions, premiums,
fund-raising, or educational use. For details, contact:
DK Publishing Special Markets, 375 Hudson Street,
New York, New York 10014 or SpecialSales@dk.com.

Color reproduction by Media Development Printing Ltd, UK

Printed and bound in Singapore by Tien Wah Press

Content previously published in
Illustrated Step-by-Step Baking

Discover more at www.dk.com

Contents

Breakfast

Buttermilk Biscuits
page 130

10 MINS · 15 MINS

Pane al latte
page 164

30 MINS · 20 MINS

Blueberry Pancakes
page 132

10 MINS · 15–20 MINS

Banana, Yogurt, and Honey Pancake Stack page 136

10 MINS · 15–20 MINS

Croissants
page 176

1 HOUR · 15–20 MINS

Croissants aux amandes
page 179

1 HOUR · 15–20 MINS

Danish Pastries
page 180

30 MINS · 15–20 MINS

Almond Crescents
page 182

30 MINS · 15–20 MINS

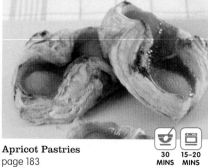

Apricot Pastries
page 183

30 MINS · 15–20 MINS

Bagels page 50

40 MINS · 25–25 MINS

Pains au chocolat
page 178

1 HOUR · 15–20 MINS

Multi-grain Breakfast Bread
page 36

45–50 MINS · 40–45 MINS

Afternoon Tea

Bara Brith
page 170

40 MINS · 25–40 MINS

English Muffins
page 30

25–30 MINS · 13–16 MINS

Cinnamon Rolls
page 172

40 MINS · 25–30 MINS

Oatcakes
page 114

20 MINS · 15 MINS

Crumpets
page 138

10 MINS · 20–26 MINS

Hot Crossed Buns
page 175

30 MINS · 15–20 MINS

Brioche Buns
page 158

40–50 MINS · 15–20 MINS

Chelsea Buns
page 174

30 MINS · 30 MINS

A Meal In Itself

Four Seasons Pizza
page 82

40 MINS   40 MINS

**Three Pepper Calzone
with Cheese** page 86

25 MINS   15–20 MINS

Pissaladière
page 88

20 MINS   1 HOUR 25 MINS

Stuffed Paratha
page 100

20 MINS   15–20 MINS

Quesadillas
page 104

5–10 MINS   30–35 MINS

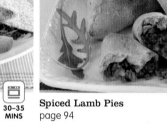

Spiced Lamb Pies
page 94

40–45 MINS   10–15 MINS

Staffordshire Oatcakes
page 144

10 MINS   15 MINS

Buckwheat Galettes page 142

25 MINS   25–30 MINS

Zweibelkuchen
page 90

30 MINS   60–65 MINS

With Drinks

Ciabatta Crostini
page 42

15 MINS · 10 MINS

Sesame Grissini
page 106

40-45 MINS · 15-18 MINS

Parmesan and Rosemary Thins page 112

10 MINS · 15 MINS

Pita Crisps
page 95

10 MINS · 7-8 MINS

Blinis
page 146

20 MINS · 15 MINS

Prawn and Guacamole Tortilla Stacks page 105

15 MINS · 10-15 MINS

Cheese Straws
page 113

10 MINS · 15 MINS

Prosciutto-wrapped Canapés page 109

45 MINS · 15-18 MINS

Soft Pretzels
page 54

50 MINS · 20 MINS

Stilton and Walnut Biscuits
page 110

10 MINS · 20 MINS

Daily Breads

RECIPE CHOOSERS

Whole Wheat Cottage Loaf
page 16

35–40 MINS 40–45 MINS

White Loaf
page 20

20 MINS 40–45 MINS

Ciabatta
page 40

30 MINS 30 MINS

Pan al latte
page 164

30 MINS 20 MINS

Pane siciliano
page 76

20 MINS 25–30 MINS

Pumpkin Soda Bread
page 122

20 MINS 50 MINS

Artisan Rye Bread
page 72

25 MINS 40–50 MINS

Pumpernickel
page 75

20 MINS 30–40 MINS

Sourdough Bread
page 63

45–50 MINS 40–45 MINS

Rosemary Focaccia
page 46
30–35 MINS · 15–20 MINS

Walnut and Rosemary Loaf
page 21
20 MINS · 30–40 MINS

Whole Wheat Baguette
page 71
20 MINS · 20–25 MINS

Challah
page 163
45–55 MINS · 35–40 MINS

Cornbread
page 126
15–20 MINS · 20–25 MINS

Hefezopf
page 160
20 MINS · 25–35 MINS

Anadama Cornbread
page 38
25 MINS · 45–50 MINS

Soda Bread
page 118
10–15 MINS · 35–40 MINS

classic breads

Whole Wheat Cottage Loaf

Stone-ground whole wheat flour can vary in its absorbency, and you may need more or less water.

MAKES 2 LOAVES · **35–40 MINS** · **40–45 MINS** · **UP TO 8 WEEKS**

Rising and proofing time
1¾–2¼ hrs

Ingredients
4 tbsp unsalted butter, plus extra for greasing
3 tbsp honey
3 tsp dried yeast
1 tbsp salt
¾ cup all-purpose flour, plus extra for dusting
5 cups stone-ground whole wheat flour

1 Melt the butter. Mix 1 tablespoon of honey and ¼ cup lukewarm water in a small bowl.

2 Sprinkle the yeast over the honey mixture. Leave it for 5 minutes to dissolve, stirring once.

3 Mix the butter, remaining honey, 1½ cups lukewarm water, yeast, and salt in a bowl.

4 Stir in the white flour with half the whole wheat flour and mix with your hands.

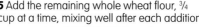

5 Add the remaining whole wheat flour, ¾ cup at a time, mixing well after each addition.

6 Stop adding wheat flour when the dough pulls away from the side of the bowl in a ball.

7 Turn the dough out onto a floured work surface and sprinkle it with white flour.

8 Knead for 10 minutes until it is very smooth, elastic, and forms a ball.

9 Grease a large bowl with butter. Put in the dough and flip it to butter the surface lightly.

10 Cover with a damp kitchen towel. Leave it in a warm place for 1–1½ hours until doubled.

11 Grease a baking sheet. Place the dough on a floured work surface and knock out the air.

12 Cover and let it rest for 5 minutes. Cut it into 3 equal pieces, then cut 1 piece in half.

13 Cover 1 large and 1 small piece of dough with a kitchen towel while shaping the others.

14 Shape 1 large piece into a loose ball. Fold in the sides, turn, and pinch to make a tight ball.

15 Flip the ball, seam side down, onto the prepared baking sheet.

16 Similarly, shape 1 small piece into a ball. Set it, seam-side down, on top of the first ball.

17 Using your forefinger, press through the center of the balls down to the baking sheet.

18 Repeat with the remaining 2 dough balls to shape a second loaf.

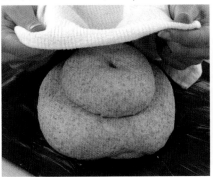

19 Cover both loaves with kitchen towels. Leave in a warm place for 45 minutes, or until doubled.

20 Preheat the oven to 375°F (190°C). Bake for 40–45 minutes, until well browned.

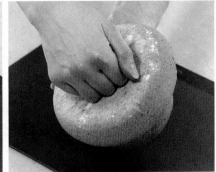

21 The loaves should sound hollow when tapped on the base. Cool on a wire rack.

Classic Loaf variations

White Loaf

Mastering a classic white loaf should be a rite of passage for all amateur bakers. Nothing beats the taste of fresh, crusty white bread, still warm from the oven.

MAKES 1 LOAF | 20 MINS | 40–45 MINS | UP TO 4 WEEKS

Rising and proofing time
2–3 hrs

Ingredients
4 cups bread flour, plus extra for dusting
1 tsp fine salt
2 tsp dried yeast
1 tbsp sunflower or vegetable oil, plus extra
  for greasing

Method
1 Put the flour and salt into a large bowl. In a small bowl, dissolve the dried yeast in 1¼ cups warm water. Once it has dissolved, add the oil. Make a well in the center of the flour. Pour in the liquid, stirring to form a rough dough. Use your hands to bring the dough together.

2 Turn the dough out onto a lightly floured work surface. Knead for 10 minutes until smooth, glossy, and elastic. Put the dough in a lightly oiled bowl, cover loosely with plastic wrap, and leave to rise in a warm place for up to 2 hours, until twice its size.

3 When the dough has risen, put it onto a floured surface and knock it back to its original size. Knead it and shape it into the desired shape; I prefer a long, curved oval shape known as a bloomer. Place the dough on a baking sheet, cover it with plastic wrap and a kitchen towel, and leave it to rise in a warm place until risen and doubled. This could take 30 minutes–1 hour. The bread is ready when it is tight and well risen, and a finger poked into the dough leaves a dent, which springs back quickly.

4 Preheat the oven to 425°F (220°C). Place one oven rack in the middle of the oven, and one below it, close to the bottom of the oven. Bring a small pan of water to a boil. Now slash the top of the loaf 2 or 3 times with a knife diagonally. This will allow the bread to continue to rise in the oven. Dust the top with flour, if wanted, and place it on the middle rack. Place a roasting pan on the bottom rack of the oven and then quickly pour the boiling water into it and shut the door. This will allow steam to be created in the oven and help the bread to rise.

5 Bake the bread for 10 minutes, then reduce to 375°F (190°C) and bake it for 30–35 minutes until the crust is golden brown and the bottom sounds hollow when tapped. Reduce to 350°F (180°C) if it is starting to brown too quickly. Remove the bread from the oven and leave to cool on a wire rack.

STORE Best eaten the day it is made, the loaf will store, well wrapped, in an airtight container overnight.

BAKER'S TIP
Tempting as it may be to taste the loaf as soon as it comes out of the oven, try to leave the bread to cool for at least 30 minutes before cutting. This will vastly improve the taste and texture of the finished loaf.

CLASSIC BREADS

Walnut and Rosemary Loaf

A perfect combination of flavors; the texture of the nuts is fabulous.

MAKES 2 LOAVES | 20 MINS | 30–40 MINS | UP TO 12 WEEKS

Proofing time
2 hrs

Ingredients
3 tsp dried yeast
1 tsp sugar
3 tbsp olive oil, plus 2 tsp extra for
  oiling and glazing
2½ cups bread flour,
  plus extra for dusting
1 tsp salt
6oz (175g) walnuts, coarsely chopped
3 tbsp finely chopped fresh rosemary

Method

1 Mix the yeast and sugar in a small bowl, then stir in ½ cup lukewarm water. Leave for 10–15 minutes, or until the mixture becomes creamy. Lightly oil a large bowl.

2 Put the flour in bowl with salt and the olive oil, then add the yeast mixture and ¾ cup water. Mix until ingredients form a dough. Knead the dough on a floured surface for 15 minutes. Knead in the walnuts and rosemary, then put the dough in the oiled bowl. Cover with a towel. Put in a warm place for 1½ hours until dough is twice its size.

3 Knock air from the dough and knead it for a few more minutes. Halve it, and shape each half into a 6in (15cm) round loaf. Cover with a towel and leave for 30 minutes to rise. Preheat oven to 450°F (230°C) and oil a large baking sheet.

4 When the dough has doubled, brush with oil and place on the baking sheet. Bake on the middle shelf for 30–40 minutes, until the loaves sound hollow when tapped on the base. Cool on a wire rack.

STORE Will keep for 1 day, wrapped in paper.

Pane di patate

Bread made with mashed potato has a soft crust and moist center. In this recipe, the dough is coated in butter and baked in a ring mold.

Rising and proofing time
1½–2¼ hrs

Special equipment
3-pint (1.75-liter) ring mold, or 10in (25cm) round cake pan, with 8oz (250ml) ramekin (optional)

Ingredients

9oz (250g) potatoes, peeled
  and cut into 2–3 pieces
2½ tsp dried yeast
9 tbsp unsalted butter,
  plus extra for greasing
1 large bunch of chives, snipped
2 tbsp sugar
2 tsp salt
2¼ cups bread flour,
  plus extra for dusting

Method

1 Place the potatoes in a saucepan with plenty of cold water. Bring to a boil and simmer until tender. Drain, reserving 1 cup of the cooking liquid. Mash with a potato masher. Let cool.

2 In a small bowl, sprinkle the yeast over ¼ cup lukewarm water. Leave for 5 minutes until dissolved, stirring once. Melt half the butter in a saucepan. Put the reserved liquid, mashed potato, dissolved yeast, and melted butter into a large bowl. Add the chives, sugar, and salt, and mix together with your hand.

3 Stir in half the flour and mix well with your hand. Add the remaining flour, ½ cup at a time, mixing well after each addition, until the dough pulls away from the sides of the bowl. It should be soft and slightly sticky. Turn the dough onto a floured work surface. Knead for 5–7 minutes, until very smooth and elastic.

4 Grease a large, clean bowl. Put the dough in the bowl and flip it so the surface is lightly buttered. Cover with a damp kitchen towel and let the dough rise in a warm place for 1–1½ hours, until doubled in size.

5 Grease the ring mold or cake pan. If using a pan, grease the outside of the ramekin and place it upside down in the center. Melt the remaining butter. Turn the dough out onto a lightly floured work surface and knock back. Cover and let rest for 5 minutes. Flour your hands and pinch off walnut-sized pieces of dough, making about 30 pieces. Roll each piece of dough into a smooth ball.

6 Put a few balls into the dish of melted butter and turn them with a spoon until coated. Transfer the balls of dough to the prepared mold or pan. Repeat with the remaining dough. Cover with a dry kitchen towel and let the loaf rise in a warm place for 40 minutes, until the mold or pan is full.

7 Preheat the oven to 375°F (190°C). Bake the bread for 40–45 minutes, until it is golden brown and starts to shrink away from the mold. Let it cool slightly on a wire rack, then carefully unmold. With your fingers, pull the bread apart while still warm.

STORE This bread is delicious still warm from the oven, but can be tightly wrapped with paper and kept for 2–3 days.

PREPARE AHEAD The dough can be made, kneaded, and left to rise in the refrigerator overnight. Shape the dough, let it come to room temperature, then bake as directed.

BAKER'S TIP

This is both a classic Italian and an American recipe, where it is known as "monkey bread." It is designed to be placed in the center of the dinner table and for diners to pull apart the sections with their fingers. It is best for a family, or more casual, gathering.

Dinner Rolls

You can shape the rolls however you like, although an assortment of different shapes looks very nice in a basket.

MAKES 16	45–55 MINS	15–18 MINS	8 WEEKS, UNBAKED

Rising and proofing time
1½–2 hrs

Ingredients
1⅛ cups milk
4 tbsp unsalted butter, cubed, plus extra for greasing
2 tbsp sugar
2½ tsp dried yeast
2 large eggs, plus 1 yolk, for glazing
2 tsp salt

4⅓ cups all-purpose flour, plus extra for dusting
poppy seeds, for sprinkling (optional)

1 Bring the milk to a boil. Put ¼ cup into a small bowl and let cool to lukewarm.

2 Add the butter and sugar to the remaining milk in the pan until melted. Cool to lukewarm.

3 Sprinkle the yeast over the ¼ cup of milk. Leave for 5 minutes to dissolve. Stir once.

4 In a large bowl, lightly beat the eggs. Add the sweetened milk, salt, and dissolved yeast.

5 Gradually stir in the flour, until the dough forms a ball. It should be soft and slightly sticky.

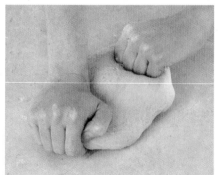

6 Knead the dough on a floured work surface for 5–7 minutes, until very smooth and elastic.

7 Put in an oiled bowl. Cover with plastic wrap. Put in a warm place for 1–1½ hours until doubled.

8 Grease two baking sheets. Put the dough on a floured work surface and knock it back.

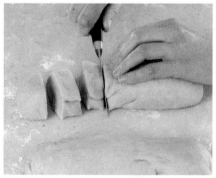

9 Cut in half and roll each piece into a cylinder. Cut each cylinder into 8 equal pieces.

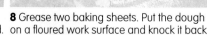

10 To shape round rolls, roll the dough in a circular motion so it forms a smooth ball.

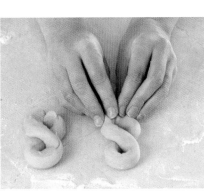

11 For a baker's knot, roll into a rope, shape into an 8, and tuck the ends through the holes.

12 For a snail, roll into a long rope and wind it around in a spiral, tucking the end underneath.

13 Put on baking sheets. Cover with a kitchen towel. Leave in a warm place for 30 minutes.

14 Preheat the oven to 425°F (220°C). Beat the egg yolk with 1 tablespoon of water.

15 Brush the rolls with the glaze and sprinkle evenly with poppy seeds, if you like.

16 Bake for 15–18 minutes until golden brown. Serve warm. **PREPARE AHEAD** These rolls can be frozen at the shaping stage, brought back to room temperature, then glazed and baked.

Bread Roll variations

Spiced Cranberry and Pecan Rolls

These sweetened, fragrant rolls were adapted from a basic white bread recipe. Try adapting your own dough with different combinations of dried fruit, nuts, seeds, and spices.

| MAKES 8 ROLLS | 20 MINS | 20–25 MINS | UP TO 4 WEEKS |

Rising and proofing time
2–3 hrs

Ingredients
4 cups bread flour, plus extra for dusting
1 tsp fine salt
1 tsp pumpkin pie spice
2 tbsp sugar
2 tsp dried yeast
²/₃ cup whole milk
½ cup dried cranberries, coarsely chopped
⅓ cup pecans, coarsely chopped
1 tbsp sunflower oil, plus extra for greasing
1 egg, beaten, for glazing

Method
1 Put the flour, salt, pumpkin spice, and sugar into a large bowl. Dissolve the yeast in ²/₃ cup warm water. Once it has dissolved, add the milk and oil. Pour the liquid into the flour mixture, stirring it together to form a rough dough. Use your hands to bring the dough together. Turn the dough out onto a floured surface. Knead the dough for 10 minutes, until it becomes smooth, glossy, and elastic.

2 Stretch the dough out thinly, scatter the cranberries and pecans over the surface, and knead for 1–2 minutes more until the added ingredients are well incorporated. Put the dough in an oiled bowl, cover with plastic wrap, and leave to rise in a warm place for up to 2 hours, until doubled.

3 Turn the dough out onto a floured work surface and gently knock it back. Knead it briefly and divide it into 8 equal-sized pieces. Shape each into a plump, round roll. Try and poke any bits of fruit or nut that are sticking out back into the rolls, as these may burn while baking.

4 Place the rolls onto a large baking sheet, cover loosely with plastic wrap and a clean kitchen towel, and leave them to rise in a warm place for 1 hour, until almost doubled in size. Preheat the oven to 400°F (200°C). Gently slash the top of the rolls in the shape of a cross with a sharp knife. This will allow the rolls to continue to rise in the oven. Lightly brush the tops with beaten egg and place them on the middle rack of the oven.

5 Bake for 20–25 minutes until golden brown and the bottoms sound hollow when tapped. Remove the rolls from the oven and leave to cool on a wire rack.

STORE These are best eaten the day they are made, but will store, well wrapped in paper, in an airtight container overnight.

> **BAKER'S TIP**
> These are a delightful alternative to traditional breakfast rolls. Try making a double quantity of the White Loaf dough (see page 20) and using half of it to make these rolls. They are especially welcome on Christmas morning, with the festive colors of the cranberries and warming fragrance of spices.

Sesame Seed Buns

These soft bread rolls are very easy to make and great for picnics or packed lunches, or for burgers at a summer barbecue.

| MAKES 8 BUNS | 30 MINS | 20 MINS |

Rising and proofing time
1½ hrs

Ingredients
2½ cups bread flour, plus extra for dusting
1 tsp salt
1 tsp dried yeast
1 tbsp vegetable oil, sunflower oil, or light olive oil, plus extra for greasing
1 egg, beaten
¼ cup sesame seeds

Method
1 Stir the flour, salt, and yeast together in a large bowl, then make a well in the middle. Pour the oil into 1½ cups tepid water, then pour this liquid into the well and quickly stir together. Leave to stand for 10 minutes.

2 Turn the dough out onto a floured surface. Knead for 5 minutes, or until smooth and elastic. Shape into a ball by bringing the edges into the middle, then turn into an oiled bowl, smooth side up. Cover with oiled plastic wrap and leave in a warm place for 1 hour, or until doubled.

3 Meanwhile, dust a baking sheet with flour. Scoop the dough onto a floured surface, dust with a little flour, then knead briefly. Pull the dough into 8 even-sized pieces, then shape into rounds. Place onto the floured baking sheet, well spaced apart, then leave for 30 minutes, or until larger and pillowy. Preheat the oven to 400°F (200°C).

4 Once risen, brush the buns with egg and sprinkle sesame seeds over each. Bake for 20 minutes, or until golden, risen, and round. Cool on a wire rack.

STORE These are best eaten the day they are made, but will store, well wrapped in paper, in an airtight container overnight.

Whole Wheat Fennel Seed Rolls

Fennel seeds and cracked black pepper make these savory rolls perfect for smoked ham sandwiches, or as buns for chorizo or pork burgers. Try experimenting with different whole spices, such as caraway or cumin.

| MAKES 6 ROLLS | 20 MINS | 25–35 MINS | UP TO 12 WEEKS |

Rising and proofing time
2 hrs

Ingredients

2 tsp dried yeast
1 tsp brown sugar
3¾ cups whole wheat flour,
  plus extra for dusting
1½ tsp fine salt
2 tsp fennel seeds
1 tsp black peppercorns, cracked
olive oil, for greasing
1 tsp sesame seeds (optional)

Method

1 Sprinkle the yeast into a small bowl, add the sugar, and mix in ⅔ cup lukewarm water. Leave for about 15 minutes for the mixture to become creamy and frothy.

2 Mix the flour with a pinch of salt in a bowl, then add the yeast mixture, and gradually add another ⅔ cup of lukewarm water. Mix until it comes together (it may need a little more water if it is too dry). Transfer to a lightly floured board and knead for about 10–15 minutes until smooth and elastic, then knead in the fennel seeds and cracked black pepper.

3 Lightly grease a bowl with olive oil. Sit the dough in the prepared bowl, cover with a kitchen towel, and leave somewhere warm for 1½ hours until doubled in size.

4 Knock back the dough and knead for a few more minutes, then divide into six pieces and shape each into a roll. Place them on an oiled baking sheet, cover, and leave to rise again for about 30 minutes. Preheat the oven to 400°F (200°C).

5 Brush the rolls with a little water, then sprinkle with sesame seeds (if using) and bake for about 25–35 minutes until the rolls are golden and sound hollow when tapped on the base. Allow to cool on the baking sheet for a few minutes, then transfer to a wire rack to cool completely.

STORE These are best eaten the day they are made, but will store, well wrapped in paper, in an airtight container overnight.

Pão de queijo

These unusual miniature cheese rolls, crisp on the outside and chewy on the inside, are a popular Brazilian street food.

MAKES 16	10 MINS	30 MINS	8 WEEKS, UNBAKED

Special equipment
food processor with blade attachment

Ingredients
½ cup milk
3–4 tbsp sunflower or vegetable oil
1 tsp salt
1⅔ cups tapioca or cassava flour, plus extra for dusting
2 large eggs, beaten, plus extra for glazing
5oz (125g) Parmesan cheese, grated

Method

1 Put the milk, ½ cup water, sunflower oil, and salt in a small saucepan and bring to a boil. Put the flour into a large bowl and quickly mix in the hot liquid. The mixture will be very clumpy and stuck together. Put it aside to cool.

2 Preheat the oven to 375°F (190°C). Once the tapioca mixture has cooled, put it into a food processor. Add the eggs and process until all the lumps disappear, and it resembles a thick, smooth paste. Add the cheese and process together until it begins to form a sticky, elastic dough.

3 Turn the mixture out onto a well-floured work surface and knead for 2–3 minutes, until it is smooth and pliable. Divide the mixture into 16 equal pieces. Roll each piece into golf ball-sized balls and place, spaced apart, on a baking sheet lined with parchment paper.

4 Brush the balls with a little beaten egg and bake in the middle of the oven for 30 minutes, until well risen and golden brown. Remove them from the oven and cool for a few minutes before eating. These are best eaten the same day they are made, preferably still warm from the oven.

PREPARE AHEAD These can be open frozen on the baking sheet at the end of step 3 and transferred to freezer bags. Simply defrost for 30 minutes and bake as usual.

BAKER'S TIP
These classic Brazilian cheese rolls are made from manioc, tapioca, or cassava flour, and are thus wheat-free. The flour clumps when mixed with the liquid at first, but the use of a food processor will help enormously here. You will find that it soon forms a smooth mass.

English Muffins

This soft, traditional English teatime bread crossed the Atlantic to become an American brunch favorite.

MAKES 10	25–30 MINS	13–16 MINS

Rising and proofing time
1½ hrs

Ingredients

2½ cups all-purpose flour,
 plus extra for dusting
1 tsp quick-rising dried yeast
1 tsp salt
2 tbsp unsalted butter, melted,
 plus extra for greasing
vegetable oil, for greasing
2 tbsp ground rice or semolina

Method

1 Pour 1¼ cups tepid water into a bowl, sprinkle in the yeast, and leave for 5 minutes to dissolve, stirring once. Mix the flour and salt in a large bowl. Make a well and pour in the yeast mixture and melted butter. Gradually draw in the flour to form a soft, pliable dough.

2 Knead the dough on a lightly floured surface for 5 minutes. Shape it into a ball and place in a large greased bowl. Cover with oiled plastic wrap and leave in a warm place for 1 hour, or until doubled in size.

3 Lay a kitchen towel on a sheet, and scatter with most of the ground rice. Turn the dough out onto a floured surface, knead briefly, and divide it into 10 balls.

Place the balls on the towel and press them into flattish rounds. Sprinkle with the rest of the ground rice and cover with another kitchen towel. Leave to rise for 20–30 minutes, or until risen.

4 Heat a large, lidded frying pan and cook the muffins in batches. Cover with the lid and cook very gently for 10–12 minutes, or until they puff up and the undersides are golden and toasted. Turn over and cook for 3–4 minutes, or until golden underneath. Cool on a wire rack. Great split, toasted, and spread with butter and jam, or as the base for eggs Benedict.

BAKER'S TIP

Homemade English muffins are far superior to anything you can buy, so it really is worth the extra effort of making them. Prepare the dough in the morning, and you can enjoy a freshly cooked batch for afternoon tea. Alternatively, leave to rise overnight, ready to bake for a leisurely breakfast.

Seeded Rye Bread

A crusty loaf accented by aromatic caraway seeds. Low-gluten rye is mixed with white flour to lighten it.

MAKES 1 LOAF | 35–40 MINS | 50–55 MINS | UP TO 8 WEEKS

Rising and proofing time
2¼–2¾ hrs

Ingredients
2½ tsp dried yeast
1 tbsp molasses
1 tbsp vegetable oil, plus extra
  for greasing
1 tbsp caraway seeds
2 tsp salt
8oz (250ml) lager
2½ cups rye flour

1¼ cups all-purpose flour,
  plus extra for dusting
polenta, for dusting
1 egg white, for glazing

1 Put the dissolved yeast, molasses, two-thirds of the caraway seeds, salt, and oil into a bowl.

2 Pour in the lager. Stir in the rye flour and mix together well with your hands.

3 Gradually add the all-purpose flour until it forms a soft, slightly sticky dough.

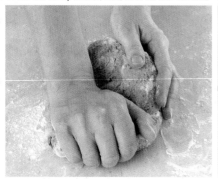

4 Knead for 8–10 minutes, until the dough is smooth and elastic. Put in an oiled bowl.

5 Cover with a damp kitchen towel. Leave in a warm place for 1½–2 hours, until doubled.

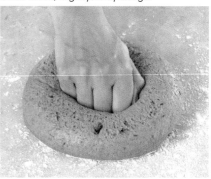

6 Sprinkle a baking sheet with polenta. Knock back the dough on a floured work surface.

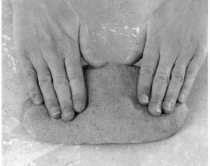

7 Cover and let it rest for 5 minutes. Pat the dough into an oval, about 10in (25cm) long.

8 Roll it back and forth on the work surface, exerting pressure on the ends to taper them.

9 Transfer to the baking sheet. Cover and leave in a warm place for 45 minutes until doubled.

10 Preheat the oven to 375°F (190°C). Beat the egg white until frothy. Brush with the glaze.

11 Sprinkle with the remaining caraway seeds and press them into the dough.

12 With a sharp knife, make 3 diagonal slashes, about ¼in (5mm) deep, on top.

13 Bake for 50–55 minutes, until well browned. The bread should sound hollow when tapped on the base. Transfer to a wire rack and cool completely. **STORE** This loaf will keep, tightly wrapped in paper, for 2 days.

Rye Bread variations

Apricot and Pumpkin Seed Rolls

Rye flour is very dense, so mix it with bread flour for a lighter texture.

MAKES 8 ROLLS | **20 MINS** | **30 MINS** | **UP TO 4 WEEKS**

Rising and proofing time
up to 4 hrs

Ingredients
2½ tsp dried yeast
1 tbsp molasses
1 tbsp sunflower or vegetable oil, plus extra for greasing
2½ cups rye flour
2 cups bread flour, plus extra for dusting
1 tsp fine salt
½ cup dried apricots, coarsely chopped
¼ cup pumpkin seeds, lightly toasted
1 egg, beaten, for glazing

Method

1 Dissolve the dried yeast in 1¼ cups warm water. Add the molasses and oil and whisk well to dissolve the molasses evenly. Put the two types of flour and the salt into a large bowl or the bowl of a electric mixer fitted with a dough hook.

2 Gradually pour the liquid into the flour mixture, stirring it to form a rough dough. Turn the dough out onto a floured work surface. Knead the dough for up to 10 minutes, or 5–7 minutes in an electric mixer on medium speed, until elastic.

3 Stretch the dough out thinly, scatter the apricots and pumpkin seeds over the surface, and knead for a minute or two more until well incorporated. Put into a lightly oiled bowl, cover loosely with plastic wrap, and leave to rise in a warm place for up to 2 hours, until well risen. This dough will not double in size, as rye flour is very low in gluten, and rises slowly.

4 Turn it out onto a lightly floured work surface and gently knock it back. Knead it briefly and divide it into 8 equal sized

pieces. Shape each into a plump, round shape. Try and poke any bits of fruit or seed that are sticking out back into the rolls, as these may burn easily when baking.

5 Place the rolls onto a baking sheet, cover loosely with plastic wrap and a kitchen towel, and leave to rise in a warm place until well risen. This could take up to 2 hours. The rolls are ready to bake when they are tight and well risen, and a finger poked into the dough leaves a dent, which springs back quickly.

6 Preheat the oven to 375°F (190°C). Brush the rolls with beaten egg and bake in the middle of the oven for 30 minutes until golden brown and the bottoms sound hollow when tapped. Remove the rolls from the oven and leave to cool on a wire rack.

STORE These are best eaten the same day, but will store overnight, well wrapped.

ALSO TRY...

Walnut Rye Bread Toast 2½oz (75g) walnuts by dry frying in a pan for 3–4 minutes. Rub in a clean kitchen towel to remove excess skin and coarsely chop, then scatter the nuts over the thinly stretched dough instead of the apricots and pumpkins. Once risen, shape into a single ball-shaped loaf, tucking the sides under the center of the dough to get a tight, even shape, leaving the seam at the bottom; this is known as a boule. After it has risen a second time, bake for 45 minutes.

BAKER'S TIP
Here I have used apricot and pumpkin seeds, but dried cranberries, raisins, or blueberries would all work well, too. As an extra alternative, you could also try other seeds, such as sesame or poppy seeds.

Pesto Garland Bread

A loaf lightly flavored with rye and spread with fragrant homemade pesto, this bread is perfect for serving at a buffet lunch or taking on a picnic, as the slices can be pulled off in individual portions. It also looks amazing!

MAKES 1 LOAF | **35–40 MINS** | **30–35 MINS**

Rising and proofing time
1¾–2¼ hrs

Special equipment
food processor with blade attachment

Ingredients
2½ tsp dried yeast
¾ cup rye flour
1½ cups all-purpose flour, plus extra for dusting
2 tsp salt
extra virgin olive oil for greasing and glazing
leaves from 1 large bunch of basil
3 garlic cloves, peeled
3 tbsp olive oil
⅓ cup pine nuts, coarsely chopped
2oz (60g) freshly grated Parmesan cheese
freshly ground black pepper

Method

1 In a small bowl, sprinkle the yeast over ¼ cup taken from 1¼ cups lukewarm water. Let stand for about 5 minutes, until dissolved, stirring once. Put the rye flour and half the all-purpose flour in the bowl of a food processor with the salt. Combine the yeast and remaining water and pour in, blending just until mixed. Add the remaining flour, ½ cup at a time. Mix after each addition, until the dough is soft and slightly sticky.

2 Continue working the dough for 60 seconds, until elastic. Turn onto a floured work surface and remove the blade. Shape into a ball. Place in an oiled bowl. Cover with a damp kitchen towel and let rise in a warm place for 1–1½ hours, until doubled in bulk.

3 Pulse the basil and garlic in the food processor. Work until coarsely chopped. With the blades turning, gradually add 3 tablespoons oil until smooth. Transfer the pesto to a bowl and stir in the pine nuts, Parmesan, and plenty of black pepper.

4 Brush a baking sheet with oil. Place the dough onto a floured surface and knead to knock out the air. Cover and let rest for about 5 minutes. Flatten the dough, then roll it into a 16 x 12in (40 x 30cm) rectangle with a rolling pin. Spread the pesto evenly over the dough, leaving a ½in (1cm) border. Starting with a long end, roll up the rectangle into an even cylinder. Running the length of the cylinder, pinch the seam firmly together. Do not seal the ends.

5 Transfer the cylinder, seam-side down, to the baking sheet. Curve it into a ring, sealing the ends. With a sharp knife, make a series of deep cuts around the ring, about 2in (5cm) apart. Pull the slices apart slightly and twist them over to lie flat. Cover with a dry kitchen towel and let rise in a warm place for about 45 minutes, until doubled in bulk.

6 Preheat the oven to 425°F (220°C). Brush the loaf with oil. Bake for 10 minutes. Reduce to 375°F (190°C), and bake for 20–25 minutes, until golden. Cool slightly on a wire rack. Serve the same day.

Multi-grain Breakfast Bread

This hearty bread combines rolled oats, wheat bran, polenta, whole wheat and all-purpose flours, with sunflower seeds for added crunch.

MAKES 2 LOAVES · **45–50 MINS** · **40–45 MINS** · **UP TO 8 WEEKS**

Rising and proofing time
2½–3 hrs

Ingredients
¾ cup sunflower seeds
1½ cups buttermilk
2½ tsp quick-rising dried yeast
½ cup rolled oats
⅓ cup wheat bran
½ cup polenta or fine yellow cornmeal, plus extra for dusting
¼ cup brown sugar
1 tbsp salt
2 cups whole wheat flour
2 cups all-purpose flour, plus extra for dusting
unsalted butter, for greasing
1 egg white, beaten, for glazing

Method

1 Preheat the oven to 350°F (180°C). Spread the seeds on a baking sheet and toast in the oven until lightly browned. Let cool, then coarsely chop.

2 Pour the buttermilk into a saucepan and heat to just lukewarm. Sprinkle the yeast over ¼ cup lukewarm water. Set aside for 2 minutes, stir gently, then leave for 2–3 minutes, until completely dissolved.

3 Put the sunflower seeds, rolled oats, wheat bran, polenta, brown sugar, and salt in a large bowl. Add the dissolved yeast and buttermilk and mix together. Stir in the whole wheat flour with half the all-purpose flour and mix well with your hand.

4 Add the remaining all-purpose flour, ½ cup at a time, mixing well after each addition, until the dough pulls away from the sides of the bowl in a ball. It should be soft and slightly sticky. Turn the dough onto a floured work surface. Knead for 8–10 minutes, until it is very smooth, elastic, and forms into a ball.

5 Grease a large bowl with butter. Put the dough in the bowl and flip it so the surface is lightly buttered. Cover with a damp kitchen towel and leave to rise in a warm place for 1½–2 hours, until doubled in size.

6 Sprinkle 2 baking sheets with polenta. Turn the dough out onto a lightly floured work surface and knock back. Cover and let it rest for 5 minutes. With a sharp knife, cut the dough in half. Shape each half into a thin oval. Cover with a dry kitchen towel and leave to rise in a warm place for 1 hour, or until doubled in size again.

7 Preheat the oven to 375°F (190°C). Brush the loaves with egg white and bake for 40–45 minutes, until the base of the loaves sound hollow when tapped. Transfer the loaves to a wire rack to cool completely.

STORE This bread is best on the day of baking, but can be tightly wrapped in paper and kept for 2–3 days.

BAKER'S TIP

Buttermilk is a great ingredient for bakers. Try adding it to any baking recipe that calls for milk. Its mild acidity brings a slight tang of sourness, while its active ingredients will lighten and soften the texture of most baked goods. You can find it in most supermarkets.

CLASSIC BREADS

Anadama Cornbread

This dark, sweet cornbread originally hails from New England. It is curiously sweet and savory at the same time, and keeps very well.

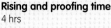

MAKES 1 LOAF | 25 MINS | 45–50 MINS | UP TO 8 WEEKS

Rising and proofing time
4 hrs

Ingredients

½ cup milk
½ cup polenta or fine yellow cornmeal
4 tbsp unsalted butter, softened
½ cup molasses
2 tsp dried yeast
2½ cups all-purpose flour, plus extra for dusting
1 tsp salt
vegetable oil, for greasing
1 egg, beaten, for glazing

Method

1 Heat ½ cup water and the milk in a small saucepan. Bring to a boil and add the polenta. Cook for a minute or two until it thickens, then remove from the heat. Add the butter and stir until it is well mixed. Beat in the molasses, then set aside to cool.

2 Dissolve the yeast in ⅓ cup warm water and stir well. Put the flour and salt into a bowl and make a well. Gradually stir in the polenta mixture, then add the yeast mixture to make a soft, sticky dough.

3 Turn the dough out onto a lightly floured work surface. Knead for about 10 minutes, until soft and elastic. It will remain fairly sticky, but should not stick to your hands. Knead in a little flour if it seems too wet. Put the dough in a lightly oiled bowl, cover loosely with plastic wrap, and leave to rise in a warm place for up to 2 hours. The dough will not double in size, but should be very soft and pliable when well risen.

4 Turn the dough out onto a lightly floured work surface and gently knock it back. Knead it briefly and shape it into a flattened oval, tucking the sides underneath the center of the dough to get a tight, even shape. Place on a large baking sheet and cover loosely with plastic wrap and a clean kitchen towel. Leave it to rise in a warm place for about 2 hours. The dough is ready to bake when it is tight and well risen, and a finger gently poked into the dough leaves a dent, which springs back quickly.

5 Preheat the oven to 350°F (180°C). Place one oven rack in the middle of the oven, and one below it, close to the bottom. Bring a small pan of water to a boil. Brush the loaf all over with a little beaten egg, and gently slash the top 2–3 times with a sharp knife diagonally. This will alllow the bread to continue to rise in the oven. Dust the top with a little flour, if desired, and place it on the middle shelf. Place a roasting pan on the bottom shelf, then quickly pour the boiling water into it and shut the door.

6 Bake for 45–50 minutes, until the crust is nicely darkened and the bottom sounds hollow when tapped. Remove from the oven and leave to cool on a wire rack.

STORE The bread will keep, well wrapped in paper, in an airtight container for 5 days.

BAKER'S TIP

Slashing the loaf allows the bread to continue rising in the oven, as does the steam from the pan of boiling water, which also helps to give the bread a good crust. Anadama tastes wonderful with Emmental or Gruyère, or simply buttered and topped with some good ham and a little mustard.

CLASSIC BREADS

Ciabatta

One of the simplest breads to master, a good ciabatta should be well risen and crusty, with large air pockets.

MAKES 2 LOAVES | **30 MINS** | **30 MINS** | **UP TO 8 WEEKS**

Rising and proofing time
3 hrs

Ingredients
2 tsp dried yeast
2 tbsp olive oil,
  plus extra for greasing
2½ cups bread flour, plus extra
  for dusting
1 tsp sea salt

1 Dissolve the yeast in 1½ cups warm water. Once it has dissolved, add the oil.

2 Put the flour and salt in a bowl. Make a well, pour in the yeast, and stir to form a soft dough.

3 Knead on a floured surface for 10 minutes, until smooth, soft, and somewhat slippery.

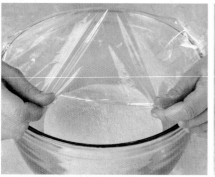

4 Put the dough in a lightly oiled bowl and cover loosely with plastic wrap.

5 Leave to rise in a warm place for 2 hours until doubled. Turn out onto a floured surface.

6 Gently knock back the dough with your fists, then divide it into 2 equal pieces.

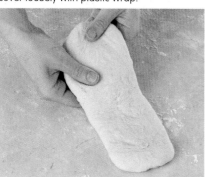

7 Knead them briefly and shape into traditional slipper shapes, around 12 x 4in (30 x 10cm).

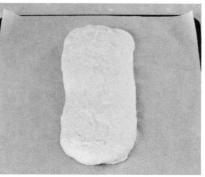

8 Place each loaf on a lined baking sheet with enough space around to allow it to expand.

9 Cover loosely with plastic wrap and a towel. Leave for 1 hour until doubled in volume.

CLASSIC BREADS

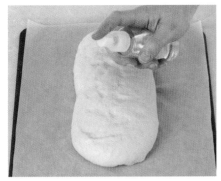

10 Preheat the oven to 450°F (230°C). Spray the loaves with a fine mist of water.

11 Bake on the middle rack for 30 minutes, spraying them with water every 10 minutes.

12 It is cooked when the top is golden brown and the base sounds hollow when tapped.

13 When cooked, turn the loaves out onto a wire rack to cool for at least 30 minutes before cutting. **STORE** These are best eaten the same day, but can be stored overnight, wrapped in paper.

Ciabatta variations

Green Olive and Rosemary Ciabatta

Green olives and rosemary make a vibrant alternative to plain ciabatta.

MAKES 2 LOAVES | 40 MINS | 30 MINS | UP TO 8 WEEKS

Rising and proofing time
3 hrs

Ingredients
1 quantity ciabatta dough,
   see page 40, steps 1–3
4oz (100g) good-quality pitted green olives,
   drained, roughly chopped
2 good sprigs of rosemary, leaves only,
   coarsely chopped

Method
1 Knead the dough for 10 minutes. Then stretch it out thinly on the work surface, scatter evenly with the olives and rosemary, and bring the sides together to cover the ingredients. Knead the dough until well incorporated. Put it in an oiled bowl, cover with plastic wrap, and leave to rise in a warm place for up to 2 hours, until doubled.

2 Turn the dough out onto a floured work surface and knock it back. Divide it into two equal pieces. Knead the pieces and shape them into two traditional slipper shapes, each 12 x 4in (30 x 10cm). Put each loaf on a lined baking sheet with enough space around it to allow it to expand as it rises. Cover with plastic wrap and a kitchen towel and leave for 1 hour until twice its volume.

3 Preheat the oven to 450°F (230°C). Spray the loaves with a fine mist of water and bake in the center of the oven for 30 minutes until golden brown; spray the loaves with water every 10 minutes. The bread is cooked when the underneath sounds hollow when tapped. Cool on a wire rack for 30 minutes before cutting.

STORE Best eaten on the same day. Can be stored overnight, wrapped in paper.

Ciabatta Crostini

Don't waste day-old ciabatta; slice it and bake the slices to make crostini, which will keep for days and can be used for snacks, canapés, or croutons. ▶

MAKES 25–30 | 15 MINS | 10 MINS

Ingredients
1 loaf day-old ciabatta bread, see pages 40–41
olive oil

For the toppings
½ cup arugula pesto, or 4oz (100g) roasted red peppers, sliced and mixed with chopped basil, or ½ cup black olive tapenade topped with 4oz (100g) goat cheese

Method
1 Preheat the oven to 425°F (220°C). Slice the ciabatta into ½in (1cm) slices. Brush the tops with olive oil.

2 Bake them on the top rack for 10 minutes, turning them after 5 minutes. Remove from the oven and cool on a wire rack.

3 Once cooled, top with any of the three suggested toppings, just before serving. If using the tapenade and goat cheese topping, briefly grill before serving.

PREPARE AHEAD The baked, unadorned crostini will keep in an airtight container for 3 days. Add the topping just before serving.

Black Olive and Peppadew Ciabatta

Try using black olives and Peppadew peppers for a delicious ciabatta loaf studded with red and black. **PICTURED OVERLEAF**

MAKES 2 LOAVES | 40 MINS | 30 MINS | UP TO 8 WEEKS

Rising and proofing time
3 hrs

Ingredients
1 quantity ciabatta dough,
   see page 40, steps 1–3
2oz (50g) pitted black olives, drained, coarsely chopped
2oz (50g) Peppadew small red peppers, drained, coarsely chopped

Method
1 Once the dough has been kneaded for 10 minutes, stretch it out thinly on the work surface, scatter with the olives and peppers, and bring the sides together to cover the ingredients. Knead the dough briefly until they are incorporated. Put the dough in an oiled bowl, cover loosely with plastic wrap, and leave to rise in a warm place for up to 2 hours, until doubled in size.

2 Turn the dough out onto a floured work surface and knock it back. Divide it into two pieces. Knead the pieces and shape them into two slipper shapes, each 12 x 4in (30 x 10cm). Place each loaf on a lined baking sheet. Cover with plastic wrap and a kitchen towel and leave for an hour until doubled.

3 Preheat the oven to 450°F (230°C). Mist the bread with water and bake in the center of the oven for 30 minutes until golden brown. Mist every 10 minutes. The bread is cooked when the base sounds hollow when tapped. Cool for 30 minutes before cutting.

STORE Best eaten on the same day. Can be stored overnight, wrapped in paper.

BAKER'S TIP
Ciabatta dough should be wet and loose on kneading, as this will help to create the large air pockets traditionally found in the finished loaf. Wet doughs are easier to knead in a machine fitted with a dough hook, as they are a little sticky to manage well with your hands.

Rosemary Focaccia

A good-tempered dough that can be left in the refrigerator to rise overnight. Bring back to room temperature to bake.

SERVES 6–8 | 30–35 MINS | 15–20 MINS

Rising and proofing time
1½–2¼ hrs

Special equipment
15 x 9in (38 x 23cm) jelly roll pan

Ingredients
3 tsp dried yeast
2¼ cups all-purpose flour, plus extra
  for dusting
2 tsp salt
leaves from 5–7 rosemary sprigs
⅓ cup extra virgin olive oil, plus extra
  for greasing
¼ tsp freshly ground black pepper
Sea salt flakes

1 Sprinkle the yeast over 4 tablespoons of warm water. Leave for 5 minutes, stirring once.

2 In a large bowl, mix the flour with the salt and make a well in the center.

3 Add the chopped rosemary, 4 tablespoons oil, yeast, pepper, and 1 cup lukewarm water.

4 Gradually draw in the flour and work it into the other ingredients to form a smooth dough.

5 The dough should be soft and sticky. Do not be tempted to add more flour to dry it out.

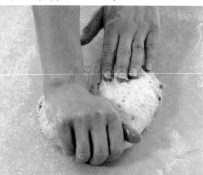

6 Sprinkle the dough with flour and knead for 5–7 minutes on a floured work surface.

7 When ready, the dough will be very smooth and elastic. Place in an oiled bowl.

8 Cover with a damp kitchen towel. Leave to rise in a warm place for 1–1½ hours, until doubled.

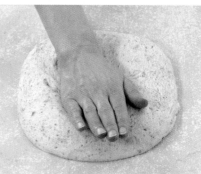

9 Put the dough on a floured work surface and knock out the air.

10 Cover with a dry kitchen towel and let it rest for about 5 minutes. Brush the pan with oil.

11 Transfer the dough to the pan. With your hands, flatten the dough to fill the pan evenly.

12 Cover with a kitchen towel and leave to rise in a warm place for 35–45 minutes, until puffed.

13 Preheat the oven to 400°F (200°C). Scatter the reserved rosemary leaves on top.

14 With your fingertips, poke the dough all over to make deep dimples.

15 Pour spoonfuls of the remaining oil all over the dough and sprinkle with the salt flakes.

16 Bake on the top rack for 15–20 minutes, until browned. Transfer to a wire rack. **ALSO TRY...**
Sage Focaccia Omit rosemary and black pepper at step 3. Add 3–5 sage sprigs, chopped.

Focaccia variations

Blackberry Focaccia

A sweet twist on a classic bread, perfect for a late summer picnic.

SERVES 6–8 | 30–35 MINS | 15–20 MINS

Rising and proofing time
1½–2¼ hrs

Special equipment
15 x 9in (38 x 23cm) jelly roll pan

Ingredients
1 tbsp dried yeast
2¼ cups all-purpose flour,
  plus extra for dusting
1 tsp salt
2 tbsp sugar, plus 1 tbsp for sprinkling
⅓ cup extra virgin olive oil,
  plus extra for greasing
10oz (300g) blackberries

Method

1 In a small bowl, sprinkle the yeast over 4 tablespoons lukewarm water. Let stand for 5 minutes until dissolved, stirring once.

2 In a large bowl, mix the flour with the salt and 2 tablespoons of the sugar. Make a well in the center and add the dissolved yeast, 4 tablespoons of the oil, and 1 cup lukewarm water. Draw in the flour and mix to form a smooth dough. The dough should be soft and sticky; avoid adding more flour to dry it out.

3 Flour your hands and the dough, and turn it out onto a floured surface. Knead for 5–7 minutes, until smooth and elastic. Transfer to an oiled bowl and cover with a damp kitchen towel. Leave to rise in a warm place until doubled in bulk; about 1–1½ hours.

4 Generously brush the pan with olive oil. Turn out the dough and knock out the air. Cover with a dry kitchen towel and leave to rest for 5 minutes. Transfer to the pan, flattening with your hands to fill it. Scatter the blackberries over the surface of the dough, cover, and leave to rise in a warm place for 35–45 minutes, until puffed.

5 Preheat the oven to 400°F (200°C). Brush the dough with the remaining oil and sprinkle with the rest of the sugar. Bake in the top of the oven for 15–20 minutes, until lightly browned. Cool slightly on a wire rack, then serve warm.

PREPARE AHEAD After kneading, at the end of step 3, the dough can be loosely covered with plastic wrap and left to rise in the refrigerator overnight.

Fougasse

Fougasse is the French equivalent of the Italian focaccia, most associated with the region of Provence. The traditional leaf effect is surprisingly easy to achieve and looks lovely.

MAKES 3 LOAVES   **30–35 MINS**   **15 MINS**

Rising and proofing time
6 hrs

Ingredients
5 tbsp olive oil, plus extra for greasing
1 onion, finely chopped
2 strips bacon, finely chopped
3 cups bread flour, plus extra for dusting
1/4 oz (7.5g) packet dried yeast
1 tsp salt
sea salt flakes, for sprinkling

Method

1 Heat 1 tbsp of the oil in a frying pan. Cook the onion and bacon until browned, remove from the pan, and set aside.

2 Mix 1½ cups of the flour with the yeast. Add about ⅔ cup water, then mix for 3–4 minutes. Cover and leave to rise and then fall again. This should take about 4 hours.

3 Add the remaining flour, the salt, ⅔ cup water, and the remaining ¼ cup olive oil, and mix well. Turn out onto a lightly floured work surface and knead to a smooth dough. Return to the bowl to rise for 1 hour, or until doubled in size.

4 Line 3 baking sheets with parchment paper. Punch down the dough, then add the onion and bacon. Knead well, then divide the dough into 3 balls. Flatten each ball to about 1in (2.5cm) high with a rolling pin, then shape each into a rough circle.

5 Put the dough circles onto baking sheets. To create the traditional leaf shapes, cut each circle with a sharp knife, twice down the center, then 3 times on either side on a slant. Cut all the way through the thickness of the dough, but not through the edges. Brush with olive oil, sprinkle with sea salt, and leave to rise for 1 hour, or until doubled in size. Preheat the oven to 450°F (230°C).

6 Bake the loaves for 15 minutes, until golden. Remove from the oven and allow to cool before serving.

Bagels

Making bagels is surprisingly simple. Try sprinkling with poppy or sesame seeds after brushing with egg.

MAKES 8–10	40 MINS	20–25 MINS	8 WEEKS, UNBAKED

Rising and proofing time
1½–3 hrs

Ingredients
3¼ cups bread flour, plus extra
  for dusting
2 tsp fine salt
2 tsp sugar
2 tsp dried yeast
1 tbsp sunflower or vegetable oil,
  plus extra for greasing
1 egg, beaten, for glazing

1 Put the flour, salt, and sugar in a bowl. Dissolve the yeast in 1¾ cups warm water.

2 Add the oil and pour the liquid into the flour mixture, stirring together to form a soft dough.

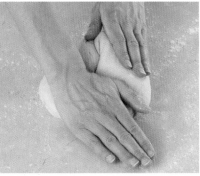

3 Knead for 10 minutes on a floured surface until smooth. Transfer to an oiled bowl.

4 Cover loosely with plastic wrap and let rise in a warm place for 1–2 hours, until doubled.

5 Transfer to a floured surface, push it down to its original size, and divide into 8–10 pieces.

6 Take each piece of dough and roll it under your palm to make a fat log shape.

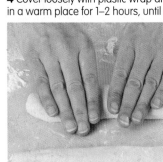

7 Using your palms, continue to roll it toward each end, until it is about 10in (25cm) long.

8 Wrap the dough around your knuckles, so the ends are underneath your palm.

9 Squeeze gently, then roll briefly to seal the end. The hole should still be big at this stage.

10 Transfer to 2 baking sheets lined with parchment. Repeat to shape all the bagels.

11 Cover with plastic wrap and a towel. Leave in a warm place until doubled; up to 1 hour.

12 Preheat the oven to 425°F (220°C) and set a large saucepan of water to boil.

13 Poach the bagels in gently simmering water for 1 minute on either side.

14 Remove them from the water with a slotted spoon. Dry them briefly on a clean kitchen towel.

15 Return the bagels to the baking sheets and brush them with a little beaten egg.

16 Bake in the center of the oven for 20–25 minutes until golden. Cool for 5 minutes on a wire rack before serving. **STORE** Best the day they are made, but still good toasted the next day.

Bagel variations

Cinnamon and Raisin Bagels

These spiced, sweet bagels are delicious fresh from the oven. Trim the crusts from any leftovers and use as an alternative for Bread and Butter Pudding (see page 168).

| MAKES 8–10 | 40 MINS | 20–25 MINS | 8 WEEKS, UNBAKED |

Rising and proofing time
1½–3 hrs

Ingredients
3¼ cups bread flour, plus extra for dusting
2 tsp fine salt
2 tsp sugar
2 tsp ground cinnamon
2 tsp dried yeast
1 tbsp sunflower or vegetable oil,
  plus extra for greasing
¼ cup raisins
1 egg, beaten, for glazing

Method
1 Put the flour, salt, sugar, and cinnamon into a large bowl. Dissolve the yeast in 1¾ cups warm water, whisking gently to help it dissolve, then add the oil. Gradually pour the liquid into the flour mixture, stirring to form a soft dough. Knead on a well floured work surface, until smooth, soft, and pliable.

2 Stretch the dough out thinly, scatter the raisins evenly over it, and knead briefly until well mixed. Put it in an oiled bowl, cover with plastic wrap, and leave to rise in a warm place for 1–2 hours, until nearly doubled.

3 Place the dough on a floured surface and gently push it down until it is back to its original size. Divide it into 8–10 equal pieces. Take each piece and roll it under your palm to make a fat log shape. Using both your palms, continue to roll the dough outward toward each end, until it is about 10in (25cm) long.

4 Wrap the dough around your knuckles, so the ends are underneath your palm. Squeeze gently, then roll the bagel briefly to seal the end. The hole should still be quite big at this stage. Transfer to 2 baking sheets lined with parchment paper and cover loosely with plastic wrap and a kitchen towel. Leave in a warm place for up to 1 hour, until well puffed up and doubled in size.

5 Preheat the oven to 425°F (220°C) and set a large pan of water to boil. Gently poach the bagels, in batches of 3 or 4, in the simmering water for 1 minute, then flip them over and poach for another minute. Remove with a slotted spoon, dry briefly on a kitchen towel, then return to the baking sheets. Brush with the beaten egg. Bake in the center of the oven for 20–25 minutes until golden brown. Remove from the oven and cool for at least 5 minutes on a wire rack before eating.

STORE Best served the day they are made, but good toasted the next day.

Mini Bagels

Great for parties, try serving halved and topped simply with cream cheese, a curl of smoked salmon, lemon juice, and a sprinkling of cracked black pepper. ▶

| MAKES 16–20 | 45 MINS | 15–20 MINS | 8 WEEKS, UNBAKED |

Rising and proofing time
1½–2½ hrs

Ingredients
1 quantity bagel dough, see page 50, steps 1–4

Method
1 When the dough has risen, place it on a floured work surface and knock it back. Divide it into 16–20 equal pieces, depending on the size you want. Take each piece and roll it under your palm to make a log shape. Use both your palms to roll the dough outward toward each end, until it is 6in (15cm) long.

2 Take the dough and wrap it around the three middle fingers of your hand, so the ends are under your palm. Pinch gently, then roll briefly to seal the end. The hole should still be big at this stage. Put the bagels on 2 baking sheets lined with parchment paper and cover with plastic wrap and a ktichen towel. Leave in a warm place for 30 minutes, until well puffed up.

3 Preheat the oven to 425°F (220°C) and set a large pan of water to boil. Gently poach the bagels in batches of 6–8, poaching each side for just 30 seconds. Briefly dry the bagels with a kitchen towel, brush with the beaten egg, and bake for 15–20 minutes until golden brown. Remove from the oven and cool for at least 5 minutes on a wire rack before eating.

STORE These mini bagels are best served fresh the day they are made, but are also good toasted the next day.

BAKER'S TIP
The secret to cooking an authentic bagel is to poach the risen bagels briefly in simmering water before baking. It is this unusual step that helps to give them their classic chewy texture and soft inside crumb.

Soft Pretzels

These German breads are great fun to make; the two-stage glazing method gives an authentic result.

MAKES 16 | 50 MINS | 20 MINS | UP TO 8 WEEKS

Rising and proofing time
1½–2½ hrs

Ingredients
2 cups bread flour, plus extra
  for dusting
1 cup all-purpose flour
1 tsp salt
2 tbsp sugar
2 tsp dried yeast
1 tbsp sunflower or vegetable oil,
  plus extra for greasing

For the glaze
¼ tsp baking soda
coarse sea salt
1 egg, beaten

CLASSIC BREADS

1 Put the two types of flour, salt, and sugar into a large bowl.

2 Sprinkle the yeast over 1¼ cups warm water. Stir, leave for 5 minutes, and add the oil.

3 Gradually pour the liquid into the flour mixture, stirring to form a soft dough.

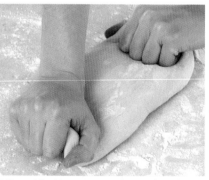

4 Knead for 10 minutes until smooth, soft, and pliable. Transfer to an oiled bowl.

5 Cover loosely with plastic wrap and leave in a warm place for 1–2 hours, until nearly doubled.

6 Turn the dough out onto a lightly floured work surface and gently knock it back.

7 Divide the dough into 16 equal sized pieces, using a sharp knife to cut it cleanly.

8 Take each piece of dough and roll it under your palm to make a log shape.

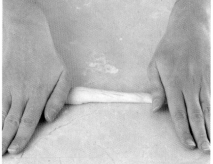

9 Using your palms, continue to roll the dough toward each end, until it is 18in (45cm) long.

10 If difficult to stretch, hold by either end and rotate in a looping action, like a jump rope.

11 Take each end of the dough and cross them over each other, forming a heart shape.

12 Now twist the ends around each other, as though they had linked arms.

13 Secure the ends to the sides of the pretzel; it will appear quite loose at this stage.

14 Repeat to make 16 pretzels, placing them on baking sheets lined with parchment.

15 Cover with plastic wrap and a towel. Leave in a warm place for 30 minutes, until puffed up.

16 Preheat the oven to 400°F (200°C). Mix the soda in 2 tablespoons boiling water.

17 Brush the pretzels with the mixture. This gives them a dark color and chewy exterior.

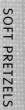

18 Scatter flakes of sea salt or sesame seeds over the brushed pretzels. Bake for 15 minutes.

19 Remove from the oven and brush with a little beaten egg. Bake for another 5 minutes.

20 Remove from the oven. The pretzels should be dark golden brown with a shiny finish.

21 Transfer to a wire rack and leave to cool for at least 5 minutes before serving.

Soft Pretzel variations

Sugar and Cinnamon Pretzels

A delicious sweet alternative to plain pretzels, these are definitely best eaten straight from the oven.
Try toasting any leftover pretzels or gently reheating in a warm oven.

MAKES 16 · **50 MINS** · **20 MINS** · **UP TO 8 WEEKS**

Rising and proofing time
1½–2½ hrs

Ingredients
1 quantity unbaked pretzels,
  see pages 56–57, steps 1–15

For the glaze
¼ tsp baking soda
1 egg, beaten
2 tbsp unsalted butter, melted
¼ cup sugar
2 tsp ground cinnamon

Method

1 Preheat the oven to 400°F (200°C). Dissolve the baking soda in 2 tablespoons boiling water and brush it all over the shaped and risen pretzels. Bake for 15 minutes. Remove from the oven, brush all over with egg, and return to the oven for 5 minutes until dark golden brown and shiny.

2 Remove the pretzels from the oven and brush each one with melted butter. Mix the sugar and cinnamon on a plate and dip the buttered side of the pretzels into the mix. Leave to cool on a wire rack for at least 5 minutes before serving.

STORE These can be stored in an airtight container overnight.

BAKER'S TIP

Pretzels get their traditional mahogany coloring and chewy texture from a quick dip in baking soda before cooking. The dough can be tricky to handle at home, so be sure to brush twice: first with the baking soda solution, and later with some beaten egg, for an easy way to perfect pretzels.

Hot Dog Pretzels

These pretzeldogs are guaranteed to be a big hit at a children's party and are simple to prepare.
Warming and festive in appearance, they are also great for a winter celebration. ▶

MAKES 8 · **30 MINS** · **15 MINS** · **UP TO 8 WEEKS**

Rising and proofing time
1½–2½ hrs

Ingredients
1 tsp dried yeast
½ tbsp sunflower or vegetable oil,
  plus extra for greasing
1 cup bread flour, plus extra for dusting
¾ cup all-purpose flour
½ tsp salt
1 tbsp sugar
8 hot dogs
mustard (optional)

For the glaze
1 tbsp baking soda
coarse sea salt

Method

1 Put the two types of flour, salt, and sugar into a bowl. Sprinkle the yeast over 1¼ cups warm water. Stir once, then leave for 5 minutes, until dissolved. Once it has dissolved, add the oil.

2 Pour the liquid into the flour mixture, stirring it together to form a soft dough. Knead by hand for 10 minutes on a floured work surface until smooth, soft, and pliable. Put in a lightly oiled bowl, cover loosely with plastic wrap, and leave in a warm place for 1–2 hours, until nearly doubled in size.

3 Turn the dough out onto a floured work surface and knock it back. Divide it into 8 equal pieces. Take each piece of dough and roll it under your palm to make a log shape. Use both your palms to continue to roll the dough outward toward each end, until it is about 18in (45cm) long. If the dough is difficult to stretch, hold it by either end and gently rotate it in a looping action as you would a jump rope.

4 Take each hot dog and, if you like mustard (and don't mind the mess) brush with a little mustard. Starting at the top, wrap the pretzel dough around it in a circular twisting motion, so that the hot dog is completely sealed in, with only the top and the bottom showing. Pinch the dough together at the top and bottom to make sure it doesn't unwrap.

5 Place on baking sheets lined with parchment paper, cover with oiled plastic wrap and a kitchen towel, and leave in a warm place for about 30 minutes, until well puffed up. Preheat the oven to 400°F (200°C).

6 Dissolve the baking soda in 1 quart boiling water in a large saucepan. Poach the hotdogs, in batches of 3, in the simmering water for 1 minute. Remove with a slotted spatula, dry briefly on a kitchen towel, and return to the baking sheets.

7 Scatter with sea salt and bake for 15 minutes until golden brown and shiny. Remove from the oven and cool on a wire rack for 5 minutes before serving.

STORE These are best eaten while still warm, but can be stored in an airtight container in the refrigerator overnight.

artisan breads

Sourdough Bread

A true sourdough starter uses naturally-occurring yeasts to ferment. Dried yeast is a bit of a cheat, but more reliable.

MAKES 2 LOAVES | 45–50 MINS | 40–45 MINS | UP TO 8 WEEKS

Fermenting time
4–6 days

Rising and proofing time
2–2½ hrs

Ingredients

For the sourdough starter
1 tbsp dried yeast
1⅓ cups bread flour

For the sponge
1⅓ cups bread flour, plus extra
    for sprinkling

For the bread
1½ tsp dried yeast
2¼ cups bread flour, plus extra
    for dusting
1 tbsp salt
vegetable oil, for greasing
polenta or fine yellow cornmeal,
    for dusting

1 Make the starter 3–5 days ahead. Dissolve the yeast in 2 cups lukewarm water.

2 Stir in the flour, and cover. Let it ferment in a warm place for 24 hours.

3 Look at the starter; it should have become frothy and have a distinct, sour odor.

4 Stir, cover, and ferment for 2–4 days longer, stirring it each day. Then use, or refrigerate.

5 To make the sponge, mix 1 cup starter with 1 cup lukewarm water in a large bowl.

6 Stir in the flour and mix vigorously. Sprinkle with 3 tablespoons flour.

7 Cover with a damp kitchen towel, and let ferment in a warm place overnight.

8 To make the bread, dissolve the yeast in ¼ cup lukewarm water. Mix into the sponge.

9 Stir in half the flour and the salt, and mix well to combine all the ingredients.

10 Gradually add the remaining flour. Mix well, until the dough forms a soft, slightly sticky ball.

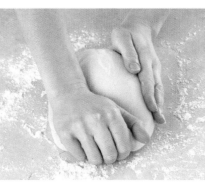

11 Knead for 8–10 minutes, until very smooth and elastic. Put in an oiled bowl.

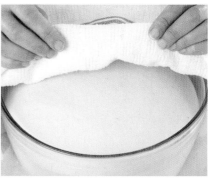

12 Cover with a damp kitchen towel and let rise in a warm place for 1–1½ hours, until doubled.

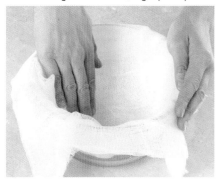

13 Line 2 x 8in (20cm) bowls with pieces of cloth, and sprinkle generously with flour.

14 Knock back the dough on a floured surface, cut in half, and shape each half into a ball.

15 Place in the bowls, covering with kitchen towels. Keep warm for 1 hour.

16 Put a pan on the oven floor and heat to 400°F (200°C). Sprinkle 2 baking sheets with polenta.

17 Turn the loaves, seam-side down, onto the baking sheets and remove the cloth.

18 With a sharp knife, make criss-cross slashes in the top of each loaf.

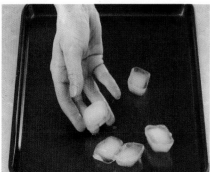

19 Put the loaves in the oven. Drop ice cubes into the roasting pan, then bake for 20 minutes.

20 Reduce to 375°F (190°C) and bake for another 20–25 minutes, until well browned.

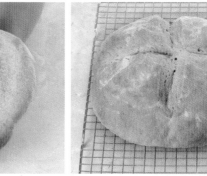

21 Transfer to a wire rack. **STORE** These can be kept for 2–3 days, tightly wrapped in paper.

Sourdough Bread variations

Sourdough Rolls

These pretty rolls are perfect for a picnic lunch.

MAKES 12 | 45–50 MINS | 25–30 MINS | UP TO 8 WEEKS

Fermenting time
4–6 days

Rising and proofing time
2–2½ hrs

Ingredients
1 quantity sourdough bread dough,
  see pages 62–63, steps 1–12

Method

1 Make the starter and the sponge; make and knead the dough, and let it rise as directed for Sourdough Bread (see page 62). Sprinkle 2 baking sheets with polenta.

2 Knock the air out of the dough and let rest as directed. Cut the dough in half. Roll 1 piece of dough into a cylinder about 2in (5cm) in diameter. With a sharp knife, cut the cylinder into 6 pieces. Repeat to shape and divide the remaining dough.

3 Lightly flour a work surface. Cup a piece of dough under the palm of your hand and roll to form a smooth ball. Repeat to shape the remaining dough. Set the rolls on the prepared baking sheets. Cover and let rise in a warm place for about 30 minutes, until doubled in size.

4 Preheat the oven to 400°F (200°C) and heat the roasting pan as directed. Lightly sprinkle each roll with flour, then, with a scalpel, make an "x" in the center of each roll. Bake as directed on page 63, until the rolls are golden and sound hollow when tapped, 25–30 minutes.

STORE The rolls will keep for 2–3 days, tightly wrapped in paper.

PREPARE AHEAD These rolls can be frozen at the shaping stage, brought back to room temperature, then glazed and baked.

Fruit and Nut Sourdough Loaf

Raisins and walnuts are a great addition to a tangy sourdough loaf. Once you've learned how to combine fruit and nuts into the dough, try experimenting with your own favorite combinations.

MAKES 2 LOAVES · **45–50 MINS** · **40–45 MINS** · **UP TO 8 WEEKS**

Fermenting time
4–6 days

Rising and proofing time
2–2½ hrs

Ingredients
1 quantity starter and sponge, see page 62, steps 1–7

For the dough
2 tsp dried yeast
1⅓ cups bread flour, plus extra for dusting
¾ cup rye flour
1 tbsp salt
¼ cup raisins
½ cup walnuts, chopped
vegetable oil, for greasing
polenta, for dusting

Method

1 Dissolve the yeast in 4 tablespoons lukewarm water. Leave for 5 minutes until frothy, then mix into the sponge. Combine the 2 types of flour and stir half the flour mix and all the salt into the sponge, mixing well to combine. Gradually add the remaining flour, mixing well, until the dough forms a soft, slightly sticky ball. Knead for 8–10 minutes, until very smooth and elastic. Flatten the dough into a rectangle, scatter over the raisins and walnuts, and bring together, kneading briefly to mix.

2 Place the dough in a large oiled bowl, cover with a damp kitchen towel, and let rise in a warm place until doubled in size; about 1–1½ hours. Line 2 x 8in (20cm) bowls with pieces of cloth, and sprinkle with flour. Knock back the dough on a floured surface, cut in half, and shape each half into a ball.

Place in the bowls, cover with dry kitchen towels, and let rise in a warm place until the bowls are full; about 1 hour.

3 Preheat the oven to 400°F (200°C) and place a roasting pan on the oven floor to heat up. Sprinkle 2 baking sheets with polenta. Turn the loaves, seam-side down, on to the sheets. With a sharp knife, make criss-cross slashes in the top of each loaf.

4 Put the loaves in the oven. Drop ice cubes into the hot roasting pan and return to the oven, then bake the bread for 20 minutes. Reduce the temperature to 375°F (190°C) and bake for another 20–25 minutes, until well browned. Transfer to a wire rack.

STORE The loaves will keep for 2–3 days, tightly wrapped in paper.

Pugliese

This classic Italian country loaf is flavored and preserved with olive oil. Do not worry if the dough seems wet at first, as the looser the dough, the larger the air pockets in the finished crumb.

MAKES 1 LOAF · **30 MINS** · **30–35 MINS** · **UP TO 4 WEEKS**

Fermenting time
12 hours or overnight

Rising and proofing time
up to 4 hours

Ingredients

For the biga
¼ tsp dried yeast
¾ cup bread flour
extra virgin olive oil, for greasing

For the dough
½ tsp dried yeast
1 tbsp extra virgin olive oil, plus extra for greasing
1⅔ cups bread flour, plus extra for dusting
1 tsp salt

Method

1 For the biga, dissolve the yeast in ½ cup warm water, whisking. Add the liquid to the flour and bring it together to form a dough. Place in an oiled bowl, cover with plastic, and put in a cool place to rise for at least 12 hours, or overnight.

2 For the dough, dissolve the yeast in ⅔ cup warm water, then add the oil. Put the biga, flour, and salt into a bowl. Add the liquid. Stir it to form a rough dough. Knead for 10 minutes on a well floured surface until smooth and elastic.

3 Put the dough in an oiled bowl, cover with plastic wrap, and leave to rise in a warm place for up to 2 hours, until doubled in size. Turn it out onto a floured surface. Gently knock it back and knead it into a shape; I like a rounded oblong.

4 Place the dough on a large baking sheet, cover with oiled plastic wrap and a kitchen towel, and leave in a warm place for up to 2 hours, until doubled in size. The bread is ready to bake when it is tight and well risen, and a finger gently poked into the dough leaves a dent that springs back quickly. Preheat the oven to 425°F (220°C).

5 Slash the loaf in a slightly off-center line. This will allow the bread to continue to rise in the oven. Dust with flour, spray with water, and place on the middle rack. Bake for 30–35 minutes. For a crisper crust, spray with water every 10 minutes. Remove the bread from the oven and let cool.

STORE The loaf will keep for 2–3 days, tightly wrapped in paper.

Baguette

Master this basic recipe and you can shape it to produce baguettes, ficelles, or bâtards whenever you like.

MAKES 2 | 30 MINS | 15–30 MINS | UP TO 4 WEEKS

Fermenting time
12 hrs or overnight

Rising and proofing time
3½ hrs

Ingredients

For the sponge
⅛ tsp dried yeast
⅓ cup bread flour
1 tbsp rye flour
vegetable oil, for greasing

For the dough
1 tsp dried yeast
1⅔ cups bread flour, plus extra for dusting
½ tsp salt

1 Dissolve the yeast in ⅓ cup warm water and add to the 2 types of flour.

2 Form a sticky, loose dough and place in an oiled bowl, with room for it to expand.

3 Cover with plastic wrap and put in a cool place to rise for at least 12 hours, or overnight.

4 To make the dough, dissolve the yeast in ⅔ cup warm water, whisking to help it dissolve.

5 Put the risen sponge, flour, and salt into a large bowl and pour in the yeast liquid.

6 Stir it all together with a wooden spoon to form a soft dough.

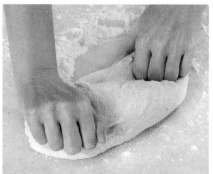

7 Knead for 10 minutes on a floured surface, until smooth, soft, glossy, and elastic.

8 Place in oiled bowl, cover with plastic wrap, and let rise in a warm place for 2 hours.

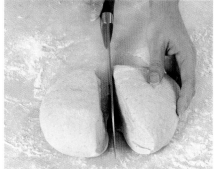

9 Place it on a floured surface. Knock it back. Divide into 2 for baguettes or 3 for ficelles.

10 Knead briefly and shape each piece into a rectangle. Tuck one short edge into the center.

11 Press down firmly, fold over the other short edge, and press firmly again.

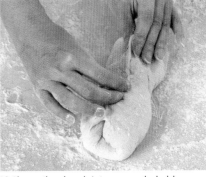

12 Shape the dough into a rounded oblong. Pinch to seal and turn seam-side down.

13 Shape into a long, thin log. A baguette is 1½in (4cm) wide, a ficelle ¾–1¼in (2–3cm).

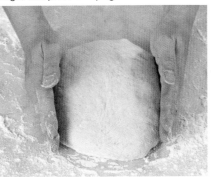

FOR A BÂTARD LOAF Knead all the dough briefly and shape it into a rough rectangle.

Tuck the furthest edge into the center, press it, then do the same with the nearest edge.

Turn it over to tuck the seam underneath and gently shape it so it tapers at the ends.

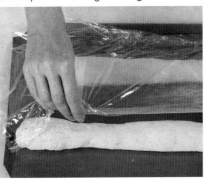

14 Put loaves on baking sheets and cover with oiled plastic wrap and a kitchen towel.

15 Keep warm for 1½ hours until doubled. Preheat the oven to 425°F (220°C).

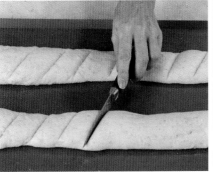

16 Slash the loaf deeply diagonally along the top, or crisscross for a bâtard.

17 Dust with a little flour, spray it with water, and place on the middle rack of the oven.

18 Bake for 15 minutes for a ficelle, 20 for a baguette, and 25–30 for a bâtard. Let it cool.

Baguette variations

Pain d'épi

This attractive variation on the baguette gets its name from its resemblance to wheat ears, *épi* in French. The wheat-ear effect is not difficult to achieve and looks very decorative. Try to eat as soon as it cools.

MAKES 3 | **40–45 MINS** | **25–30 MINS**

Rising and proofing time
4–5 hrs

Ingredients
2½ tsp dried yeast
3 cups bread flour, plus extra for dusting
2 tsp salt
unsalted butter, for greasing

Method

1 In a small bowl, sprinkle the yeast over ¼ cup lukewarm water. Let stand for 5 minutes until dissolved, stirring once.

2 Put the flour onto a work surface with the salt. Make a large well in the center and add the dissolved yeast and 1½ cups lukewarm water. Gradually draw the flour into the liquid ingredients to form a smooth dough. It should be soft and slightly sticky.

3 On a floured surface, knead the dough for 5–7 minutes, until it is very smooth, elastic, and forms a ball. Brush a bowl with melted butter. Put the dough in the bowl, and flip it so the surface is lightly buttered. Cover with a damp kitchen towel and let rise in a warm place for 2–2 ½ hours, until tripled in size.

4 Turn the dough onto a lightly floured work surface and knock back. Return to the bowl, cover, and let rise in a warm place for 1–1½ hours, until doubled in size.

5 Sprinkle a cloth with flour. Turn the dough onto a floured work surface and knock back. With a sharp knife, cut the dough into 3 equal pieces. Cover 2 pieces while shaping the other. Flour your hands and pat 1 piece of dough into a 7 x 4in (18 x 10cm) rectangle.

6 Starting with a long side, roll the rectangle into a cylinder, pinching and sealing it with your fingers as you go. Roll the cylinder, stretching it until it is a stick shape, about 14in (35cm) long. Put on the cloth. Repeat with the remaining dough, pleating the cloth between the pieces of dough.

7 Cover with a dry kitchen towel, and let rise in a warm place for 1 hour, until doubled in size. Preheat the oven to 425°F (220°C). Set a roasting pan to heat on the floor of the oven. Sprinkle 2 baking sheets with flour. Roll 2 loaves onto 1 baking sheet, placing them 6in (15cm) apart. Roll the third loaf onto the other baking sheet.

8 Make a V-shaped cut halfway through 1 of the loaves, 2-3in (5-7cm) from the end. Pull the point to the left. Make a second cut 2-3in (5-7cm) from the first, pulling to the right. Continue to shape the remaining dough. Place the loaves in the oven. At once drop ice cubes into the hot roasting pan. Bake for 25–30 minutes, until browned. Turn them over and tap the bottoms with your knuckles. The bread should sound hollow. Let cool.

Whole Wheat Baguette

Try this healthier, high-fiber alternative to a white baguette.

MAKES 2 | **20 MINS** | **20–25 MINS** | **UP TO 4 WEEKS**

Fermenting time
12 hrs or overnight

Rising and proofing time
3½ hrs

Ingredients
1 quantity sponge, see page 68, steps 1–3, substituting whole wheat for the white bread flour

For the dough
½ tsp dried yeast
¾ cup whole wheat bread flour
1¼ cups bread flour, plus extra for dusting
½ tsp salt

Method

1 To make the dough, dissolve the yeast in ⅔ cup warm water. Put the risen sponge, 2 types of flour, and salt into a large bowl. Gradually pour in the dissolved yeast, stirring together to form a dough.

2 Knead for 10 minutes on a floured work surface, until smooth, glossy, and elastic. Put the dough in a lightly oiled bowl, cover loosely with plastic, and leave in a warm place for up to 1½ hours, until doubled.

3 Turn the dough out onto a floured surface and knock it back. Divide into 2 equal pieces. Knead each piece briefly and shape it into a rough rectangle. Use your hands to tuck the furthest edge of the dough into the center, pressing it down with your fingertips, then do the same with the nearest edge. Fold the dough in half to make a long, thin oblong and press down to seal the edges.

4 Turn the dough over so the seam is underneath and use your hands to gently stretch and roll it into a long, thin log shape, no more than 1¾in (4cm) wide. Be careful not to roll it out longer than the length of a baking sheet, and bear in mind that it will expand when rising.

5 Place the loaves on 2 large baking sheets and cover loosely with oiled plastic wrap and a kitchen towel. Leave in a warm place until well risen, and almost doubled in size. This could take up to 2 hours. The bread is ready to bake when it is tight and well risen, and a finger gently poked into the dough leaves a dent that springs back quickly. Preheat the oven to 450°F (230°C).

6 Take a sharp knife and slash the top of the loaves quite deeply diagonally all along the top. This will allow the bread to continue to rise in the oven. Dust the tops with a little flour and, if you like, spray with water. Place on the middle rack of the oven, and bake for 20–25 minutes. For a crisper crust, spray the loaves with water every 10 minutes during baking. Remove the bread from the oven and cool on a wire rack.

STORE The baguette can be stored, loosely wrapped in paper, overnight.

Artisan Rye Bread

Breads made with rye flour are very popular in central and eastern Europe. This version uses a starter.

MAKES 1 LOAF **25 MINS** **40–50 MINS**

Fermenting time
overnight

Rising and proofing time
1½ hrs

Ingredients

For the starter
1 cup rye flour
⅔ cup plain yogurt
1 tsp dried yeast
1 tbsp molasses
1 tsp caraway seeds, lightly crushed

For the dough
1 cup rye flour
1½ cups bread flour,
  plus extra for dusting
2 tsp salt
vegetable oil, for greasing
1 egg, beaten
1 tsp caraway seeds, to decorate

1 In a bowl, mix all the starter ingredients together with 1 cup tepid water.

2 Cover and leave overnight. When you look at it the next day, it should be bubbling.

3 For the dough, mix the flours together with the salt, then stir into the starter.

4 Mix to make a dough, adding a little extra water if required.

5 Turn out onto a floured surface and knead for 5–10 minutes, or until smooth and springy.

6 Shape into a ball, put into an oiled bowl, and cover loosely with oiled plastic wrap.

7 Leave in a warm place for 1 hour, or until doubled in size.

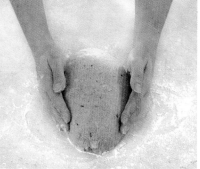

8 Flour a baking sheet. Lightly knead the dough again, then form into a football shape.

9 Lift onto the tray, re-cover it loosely, and leave to rise again for another 30 minutes.

10 Preheat the oven to 425°F (220°C). Brush the dough with the egg.

11 Immediately sprinkle evenly with the caraway seeds; they should stick to the egg.

12 Slash the loaf along its length. Bake for 20 minutes, then reduce to 400°F (200°C).

13 Bake for 20–30 minutes until dark golden. Cool on a wire rack. **STORE** Keeps well, wrapped, for 2–3 days. **ALSO TRY... Seeded Rye Bread** Knead in 4oz (100g) mixed seeds, such as pumpkin, sunflower, sesame, poppy seeds, and pine nuts, at the end of step 5.

Artisan Rye Bread variations

Hazelnut and Raisin Rye Bread

The hazelnuts and raisins in this version add a little sweetness and crunch to the bread. Try experimenting with different combinations of your own favorite nuts and dried fruit.

MAKES 1 LOAF   **25 MINS**   **40–50 MINS**   **UP TO 8 WEEKS**

Fermenting, rising, and proofing time
overnight, then 1½ hrs

Ingredients

For the starter
1 cup rye flour
⅔ cup plain yogurt
1 tsp dried yeast
1 tbsp molasses

For the dough
1 cup rye flour
1½ cups bread flour, plus extra for dusting
2 tsp salt
½ cup hazelnuts, toasted, and coarsely chopped
¼ cup raisins
vegetable oil, for greasing
1 egg, beaten

Method

1 In a bowl, mix all the starter ingredients together with 1 cup lukewarm water. Cover and leave overnight. When you look at it the next day, it should be bubbling.

2 For the dough, mix the flours together with the salt, then stir into the starter. Mix to make a dough, adding extra water if required. Turn out onto a floured surface and knead for 5–10 minutes, or until smooth and springy.

3 Stretch out the dough to a rough rectangle, scatter the hazelnuts and raisins on top, fold it over, and knead gently to incorporate. Shape into a ball and place in an oiled bowl, covered with plastic wrap. Leave in a warm place for 1 hour, until doubled in size.

4 Flour a baking sheet. Lightly knead the dough again, then form it into a shape like a football. Lift onto the sheet, cover loosely with plastic wrap, and leave to rise again for another 30 minutes.

5 Preheat the oven to 425°F (220°C). Brush the loaf with egg and slash along its length. Bake for 20 minutes. Reduce to 400°F (200°C) and bake for 20–30 minutes, until dark golden. Leave to cool on a wire rack.

STORE This rye bread will keep, wrapped in paper, for 2–3 days.

BAKER'S TIP

Rye bread makes a healthy alternative to sandwich bread. It is denser in the crumb, so makes a more substantial bite. The addition of a variety of seeds, nuts, and fruit brings crunch, extra nutrition, and texture to the finished bread. It is especially delicious with roast beef and pickles, or with cheese.

Pumpernickel

The unlikely inclusion of cocoa and coffee powder add depth of flavor.

MAKES 1 LOAF | **20 MINS** | **30–40 MINS** | **UP TO 8 WEEKS**

Fermenting, rising, and proofing time
12 hrs or overnight, then 4½ hrs

Special equipment time
1 x 9 x 5in (1-liter) loaf pan

Ingredients

For the starter
½ tsp dried yeast
½ cup rye flour
2 tbsp plain yogurt

For the dough
½ tsp dried yeast
1 tsp coffee powder
1 tbsp sunflower or vegetable oil,
   plus extra for greasing
¾ cup whole wheat flour, plus extra for dusting
¼ cup rye flour
½ tbsp cocoa powder
1 tsp salt
½ tsp caraway seeds, lightly pounded

Method

1 To make the starter, dissolve the yeast in ½ cup warm water. Put the rye flour, yogurt, and yeasted liquid in a large china or glass bowl and stir well to combine. Cover with plastic wrap, and put in a cool place to rise for at least 12 hours, or overnight.

2 To make the dough, dissolve the yeast in 3–4 tablespoons warm water. Add the coffee powder and stir until dissolved. Add the oil. Put the starter, 2 types of flour, cocoa powder, salt, and caraway seeds into a large bowl. Add the liquid.

3 Stir the ingredients, and, when it seems a little stiff, use your hands to bring the dough together. Knead for 10 minutes on a floured work surface until smooth and elastic.

4 Put the dough in a lightly oiled bowl, cover loosely with plastic wrap, and leave to rise in a warm place for up to 2 hours, until doubled in size. Turn it out onto a lightly floured work surface and gently

knock it back. Shape into a ball again, return to the bowl, and cover. Leave for another 1 hour while it rises again.

5 Turn it out onto a lightly floured work surface and knock it back again. Knead it briefly and shape it into an oblong shape. Put it into a 9 x 5in lightly oiled loaf pan, cover loosely with oiled plastic wrap and a kitchen towel, and leave it to rise in a warm place until well risen, and almost doubled in size. This could take another

1½ hours. It is ready to bake when it is tight and well risen, and a finger gently poked into the dough leaves a dent that springs back quickly. Preheat the oven to 400°F (200°C).

6 Bake in the center of the oven for 30–40 minutes until well risen and dark brown on top. Leave to cool on a wire rack.

STORE The pumpernickel keeps well, wrapped in paper, for 3 days.

Pane siciliano

This rustic semolina bread from Sicily toasts particularly well and makes deliciously crunchy bruschetta.

| MAKES 1 LOAF | 20 MINS | 25–30 MINS | UP TO 4 WEEKS |

Fermenting time
12 hrs or overnight

Rising and proofing time
2½ hrs

Ingredients

For the starter
¼ tsp dried yeast
½ cup fine semolina, or semolina flour
vegetable oil, for greasing

For the dough
1 tsp dried yeast
2 cups fine semolina, or semolina flour, plus extra for dusting
1 tsp fine salt
1 tbsp sesame seeds
1 egg, beaten, for glazing

Method

1 To make the starter, dissolve the yeast in ½ cup warm water. Add the liquid to the semolina and bring everything together to form a rough, loose dough. Place the dough in a large bowl, with plenty of room for it to expand, cover with plastic wrap, and put in a cool place to rise for at least 12 hours, or overnight.

2 To make the dough, dissolve the yeast in ¾ cup warm water. Put the risen starter, flour, and salt into a large bowl, or the bowl of an electric mixer fitted with a dough hook. Add the liquid.

3 Stir the ingredients. When it seems a little stiff use your hands to bring the dough together, or mix on a low speed. Knead by hand for up to 10 minutes, or 5–7 minutes in an electric mixer on medium speed, until smooth, glossy, and elastic.

4 Put the dough in a lightly oiled bowl, cover loosely with plastic wrap, and leave to rise in a warm place for up to 1½ hours, until doubled in size.

5 Turn the dough out onto a lightly floured work surface and gently knock it back. Knead it briefly and shape it into the desired shape; traditionally a tight boule shape. Place on a large baking sheet, cover loosely with oiled plastic wrap and a clean kitchen towel, and leave it to rise in a warm place until well risen and almost doubled in size. This could take another hour. The bread is ready to bake when it is tight and well risen, and a finger gently poked into the dough leaves a dent that springs back quickly.

6 Preheat the oven to 400°F (200°C). Brush the top of the bread with beaten egg, and scatter with the sesame seeds. Bake in the center of the preheated oven for 25–30 minutes until well risen and golden brown. Remove from the oven and transfer to a wire rack to cool for at least 30 minutes before serving.

STORE The bread can be stored, loosely wrapped in paper, for 2 days.

BAKER'S TIP

This bread can be made using either fine semolina or semolina flour. Semolina is made from durum wheat and therefore is not wheat free, but gives a deliciously rustic texture to the bread, similar to that of polenta or cornmeal. It is especially good on the side with an oil-rich tomato salad.

Schiacciata di uva

This sweet Italian "squashed" bread is very similar to a sweetened focaccia, and can be served cold or while still warm.

MAKES 1 LOAF · **25 MINS** · **20–25 MINS**

Rising and proofing time
3 hrs

Special equipment
8 x 12in (20 x 30cm) jelly roll pan
electric mixer with dough hook (optional)

Ingredients

For the dough
3¾ cups bread flour, plus extra for dusting
1 tsp fine salt
2 tbsp sugar
1½ tsp dried yeast
1 tbsp extra virgin olive oil, plus extra for greasing

For the filling
1lb 2oz (500g) small red seedless grapes, washed
3 tbsp sugar
1 tbsp finely chopped rosemary (optional)

Method

1 Put the flour, salt, and sugar into a large bowl, or the bowl of an electric mixer fitted with a dough hook. Dissolve the dried yeast in 1⅔ cups warm water. Once it has dissolved, add the oil.

2 Gradually pour the liquid into the flour mixture, stirring it together, or mixing on a low speed, to form a soft dough. Knead by hand for 10 minutes on a floured work surface, or 5–7 minutes in an electric mixer on medium speed, until smooth, glossy, and elastic. This dough should remain soft.

3 Put the dough in a lightly oiled bowl, cover loosely with plastic wrap, and leave to rise in a warm place for up to 2 hours, until doubled in size. Turn it out onto a lightly floured work surface and gently knock it back. Knead it briefly and divide it into 2 pieces, with one-third and two-thirds of the dough in each piece. Lightly oil a 8 x 12in (20 x 30cm) jelly roll pan.

4 Take the largest piece and roll it out roughly to the size of the pan. Place it in the pan and stretch it out to fill the pan, using

your fingers to mold it to the sides. Scatter two-thirds of the grapes over the surface, and sprinkle with 2 tablespoons of the sugar.

5 Now roll the smaller piece of dough out to fit on top of the grapes, stretching it with your hands if necessary. Scatter the remaining grapes on the surface of the dough, and the chopped rosemary, if using. Place the dough onto a large baking sheet, cover it loosely with lightly oiled plastic wrap and a clean kitchen towel, and leave it to rise in a warm place until well risen, and almost doubled in size. This could take up to 1 hour. Preheat the oven to 400°F (200°C).

6 Scatter the top of the risen dough with the remaining 1 tablespoon sugar, and bake for 20–25 minutes, until well risen and golden brown. Remove from the oven and leave to cool for at least 10 minutes before serving.

STORE This is best eaten the day it is made, but will store, wrapped in paper, overnight.

BAKER'S TIP

This unusual Italian flat bread is traditionally served to celebrate the grape harvest in the Tuscany region of Italy. It is best eaten the day it is made, and more or less sugar can be added to taste. It is great with cheese and, of course, with Italian red wines.

flat breads & crisp breads

Four Seasons Pizza

These pizzas have different toppings, arranged separately, to represent the four seasons. Start the day before.

MAKES 4 PIZZAS | 40 MINS | 40 MINS

Rising time
1–1½ hrs or overnight

Ingredients
2¾ cups bread flour
3 tsp dried yeast
½ tsp salt
2 tbsp extra virgin olive oil, plus extra for greasing

For the tomato sauce
2 tbsp unsalted butter
2 shallots, finely chopped

1 tbsp olive oil
1 bay leaf
3 garlic cloves, crushed
2¼lb (1kg) ripe plum tomatoes, seeded and chopped
2 tbsp tomato paste
1 tbsp sugar
sea salt
freshly ground black pepper
pinch of chili flakes (optional)

For the toppings
6oz (175g) mozzarella, thinly sliced
4oz (115g) mushrooms, thinly sliced
2 tbsp extra virgin olive oil
2 roasted red peppers, thinly sliced
8 anchovy fillets, halved lengthwise
4oz (115g) pepperoni, thinly sliced
2 tbsp capers
8 artichoke hearts, halved
12 black olives

1 Put the flour in a mixing bowl and stir in the yeast and salt.

2 Add the olive oil and 1½ cups lukewarm water, then mix to a dough.

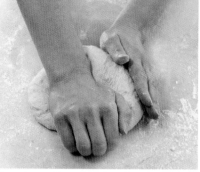

3 Knead on a floured surface for 10 minutes, or until the dough is smooth and elastic.

4 Roll the dough into a ball and place in an oiled bowl covered with oiled plastic wrap.

5 Leave in a warm place for 1–1½ hours, until doubled; or store in the refrigerator overnight.

6 For the sauce, put a saucepan over low heat. Add the butter, shallots, oil, bay leaf, and garlic.

7 Stir, cover, and cook the ingredients together for 5–6 minutes, stirring occasionally.

8 Add the tomatoes, tomato paste, and sugar. Cook for 5 minutes, stirring.

9 Now pour in 1 cup water, bring to a boil, and reduce the heat to a simmer.

10 Cook for 30 minutes, stirring, until reduced to a thick sauce. Season to taste.

11 Using a wooden spoon, press the sauce through a sieve. Cover and chill until needed.

12 To bake, preheat the oven to 400°F (200°C). Transfer the dough to a lightly floured surface.

13 Knead lightly, divide into 4, and roll or press out into 9in (23cm) rounds.

14 Grease 4 baking sheets and carefully transfer a pizza base on to each.

15 Spread the sauce over the bases, leaving a ¾in (2cm) border around the edge of each.

16 Place any leftover sauce in a small freezer-safe container and freeze for later use.

17 Top the pizzas with mozzarella, dividing it equally between the bases.

18 Arrange the mushroom slices on a quarter of each pizza and brush with the olive oil.

19 Pile the roasted pepper slices on another quarter with the anchovy fillets on top.

20 Use pepperoni and capers for the third and artichokes and olives for the fourth quarter.

21 Bake in the top of the oven, 2 at a time, for 20 minutes, or until golden brown. Serve hot.

Pizza variations

Three Pepper Calzone with Cheese

"Calzone" means "trouser leg" in Italian, perhaps due to a resemblance or because this pizza turnover could be stuffed into a roomy trouser pocket!

MAKES 4 CALZONE | **25 MINS** | **15–20 MINS**

Rising and proofing time
1½–2 hrs

Ingredients
1 quantity pizza dough, see pages 82–83, steps 1–5
¼ cup extra virgin olive oil, plus extra to serve
2 onions, thinly sliced
2 red bell peppers, cut into strips
1 green bell pepper, cut into strips
1 yellow bell pepper, cut into strips
3 garlic cloves, finely chopped
1 small bunch of any herb, such as rosemary, thyme, basil, or parsley, or a mixture, leaves finely chopped
sea salt
cayenne pepper, to taste
6oz (175g) mozzarella, sliced
all-purpose flour, for dusting
1 egg, beaten

Method

1 Heat 1 tablespoon of oil in a frying pan, add the onions, and cook, stirring, for 2–3 minutes, until soft but not brown. Transfer to a bowl and set aside. Add the remaining oil to the pan, then the peppers, garlic, and half the herbs. Season with salt and cayenne. Sauté, stirring, for 7–10 minutes, until softened but not brown. Taste for seasoning: it should be quite spicy. Add to the onions, and let cool.

2 Divide the dough into 4 equal pieces. Roll and pull each piece into a square about ½in (1cm) thick. Spoon the pepper mixture onto a diagonal half of each square, leaving a 1in (2.5cm) border. Arrange the mozzarella slices on top. Moisten the edge of each square with water, and fold 1 corner over to meet the other, forming a triangle. Pinch the edges together to seal. Put the triangles on the floured baking sheet and let rise for 30 minutes. Preheat the oven to 450°F (230°C).

3 Whisk the egg with ½ teaspoon salt, and brush over the calzone. Bake for 15–20 minutes, until golden brown. Brush each with a little olive oil, and serve.

Chicago Deep-dish Pizza

A hearty pizza, dating back to 1940s Chicago.

SERVES 4 | **35–40 MINS** | **20–25 MINS**

Rising and proofing time
1 hr 20 mins–1 hr 50 mins

Special equipment
2 x 9in (23cm) cake pans

Ingredients

For the dough
2½ tsp dried yeast
2¾ cups bread flour, plus extra for dusting
2 tsp salt
3 tbsp extra virgin olive oil, plus more for greasing
2–3 tbsp polenta

For the sauce
13oz (375g) mild Italian sausage
1 tbsp extra virgin olive oil
3 garlic cloves, finely chopped
2 x 14oz (400g) cans chopped plum tomatoes
freshly ground black pepper
leaves from 7–10 flat-leaf parsley sprigs, chopped
6oz (175g) mozzarella, torn into chunks

Method

1 In a small bowl, sprinkle the yeast over ¼ cup lukewarm water. Let stand for 5 minutes, stirring once, until dissolved. Put the flour onto a work surface with the salt. Make a large well in the center and add the dissolved yeast, 1 cup lukewarm water, and the oil. Draw in the flour and work it into the other ingredients, to form a smooth dough. It should be soft and slightly sticky.

2 Lightly flour the work surface, and knead the dough for 5–7 minutes, until very smooth and elastic. Brush a large bowl with oil. Put the dough in the bowl and flip it so the surface is lightly oiled. Cover with a damp kitchen towel and let rise in a warm place for 1–1½ hours, until doubled in size.

3 Slit the side of each sausage and push out the meat, discarding the casing. Heat the oil in a sauté pan. Add the sausage and cook over medium-high heat, breaking up

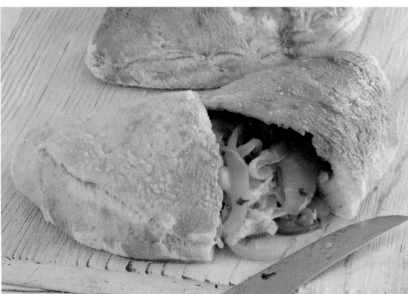

the meat with the wooden spoon, for 5–7 minutes, until cooked. Reduce the heat to medium, remove the meat from the pan, and pour off all but 1 tablespoon of the fat.

4 Stir in the garlic and cook for about 30 seconds, until fragrant. Return the sausage and stir in the tomatoes, salt, pepper, and all but 1 tablespoon of the parsley. Cook, stirring occasionally, for 10–15 minutes, until thickened. Remove from the heat, taste for seasoning, and let cool completely.

5 Brush the pans with oil. Sprinkle the polenta in the pans, and turn it to coat the bottom and side, then turn upside down and tap to remove the excess. Turn the dough onto a lightly floured work surface and knock back. Shape the dough into 2 loose balls. With a rolling pin, roll the balls into rounds to fit your pans. Working carefully, wrap the dough around the rolling pin and drape it over the pans. With your hands, press the dough into the bottom of the pans, and 1in (2.5cm) up the side, to form a rim. Cover with a dry kitchen towel, and let rise for about 20 minutes. Preheat the oven to 450°F (230°C). Heat a baking sheet in the oven.

6 Spread the sauce over the dough, leaving a border. Sprinkle with the cheese and remaining parsley. Bake for 20–25 minutes, until crisp and golden.

Pizza Bianca

This version is made without tomato sauce, kept moist with olive oil instead, and packed with fresh Mediterranean flavors.

MAKES 4 PIZZAS | 25 MINS | 20 MINS

Rising time
1–1½ hrs

Ingredients
4 pizza bases, see pages 82–83,
  steps 1–5 and 12–14
¼ cup extra virgin Italian olive oil
5oz (140g) Gorgonzola cheese, crumbled
12 slices prosciutto, torn into strips
4 fresh figs, each cut into 8 wedges, and peeled
2 tomatoes, seeded and diced
4oz (115g) arugula leaves
freshly ground black pepper

Method
1 Preheat the oven to 400°F (200°C). Place the pizza bases on the greased baking sheets. Brush with half the olive oil and scatter over the Gorgonzola cheese.

2 Bake in the oven for 20 minutes, or until the bases are crisp and turning golden. Remove from the oven.

3 Arrange the prosciutto, figs, and tomatoes on top, and return to the oven for 8 minutes, or until the toppings are just warmed and the bases are golden brown.

4 Scatter over the arugula, season with plenty of black pepper, and serve at once, drizzled with the rest of the olive oil.

BAKER'S TIP
Pizzas are delicious with or without tomato sauce. However you prefer your pizza, always remember that the toppings should be spread evenly over the base, and enough moisture added—either from tomato sauce, cheese, or good-quality extra virgin olive oil—to ensure the topping remains lubricated and appetizing.

Pissaladière

This French version of the Italian pizza derives its name from *pissala*, a paste made from anchovies.

SERVES 4	20 MINS	1 HOUR 25 MINS	UP TO 12 WEEKS

Rising time
1 hr

Special equipment
13 x 9in (32.5 x 23cm) jelly roll pan

Ingredients

For the base
1¼ cups bread flour, plus extra for dusting
sea salt
freshly ground black pepper

1 tsp brown sugar
1 tsp dried yeast
1 tbsp extra virgin olive oil, plus extra for greasing

For the topping
¼ cup extra virgin olive oil
2lb (900g) onions, finely sliced
3 garlic cloves
sprig of thyme
1 tsp herbes de Provence (dry mix of thyme, basil, rosemary, and oregano)
1 bay leaf
3½oz (140g) jar anchovies in oil
12 black pitted niçoise olives, or Italian olives

Method

1 For the base, combine the flour, 1 teaspoon salt, and black pepper to taste in a large bowl. Pour ⅔ cup lukewarm water into a separate bowl, and use a fork to whisk in the sugar, then the yeast. Set aside for 10 minutes to froth, then pour into the flour with the olive oil.

2 Mix to form a dough, adding another 2 tablespoons lukewarm water if the mixture looks too dry. Turn the dough out onto a floured board, and knead for 10 minutes, or until smooth and elastic. Shape the dough into a ball, return to a cleaned, oiled bowl, and cover with a kitchen towel. Leave in a warm place for 1 hour, or until doubled in size.

3 For the topping, put the oil in a saucepan over very low heat. Add the onions, garlic, herbs, and bay leaf. Cover and simmer gently, stirring occasionally, for 1 hour, or until the onions look like a stringy purée. Be careful not to let the onions catch; if they begin to stick, add a little water. Drain well, season with salt, and set aside, discarding the bay leaf.

4 Preheat the oven to 350°F (180°C). Knead the dough briefly on a floured surface. Roll it out so it is thin and large enough to fit the jelly roll pan. Prick all over with a fork.

5 Spread the onions over the base. Drain the anchovies, reserving 3 tablespoons oil, and slice the fillets in half lengthwise. Embed the olives in rows in the dough, and drape the anchovies in a criss-cross pattern on top of the onions. Drizzle with the reserved anchovy oil, and sprinkle with pepper.

6 Bake for 35 minutes, or until the crust is brown. The onions should not brown or dry out. Remove and serve warm, cut into rectangles, squares, or wedges, or allow to cool before serving.

BAKER'S TIP
All the elements of pissaladière are very simple, so it is imperative that you use the best-quality ingredients for the finest result. Take special care when selecting anchovies, and make sure they are packed in good-quality oil. When you can find them, smoked anchovies make an amazing substitution.

Zweibelkuchen

The combination of sour cream and caraway seeds contrast well with the sweet, melting onions used to top this traditional German tart.

SERVES 8 · 30 MINS · 60–65 MINS

Rising and proofing time
1½–2½ hrs

Special equipment
10 x 13in (26 x 32cm) rimmed baking sheet

Ingredients
4 tsp quick-rise dried yeast
3 tbsp olive oil, plus extra for greasing
3¼ cups bread flour, plus extra for dusting
1 tsp salt

For the filling
4 tbsp unsalted butter
2 tbsp olive oil
1lb 5oz (600g) onions, finely sliced
½ tsp caraway seeds
sea salt
freshly ground black pepper
½ cup sour cream
½ cup crème fraîche
3 large eggs
1 tbsp all-purpose flour
3oz (75g) bacon, cooked and crumbled

Method

1 To make the crust, dissolve the yeast in 1 cup warm water. Add the olive oil and set aside. Sift the flour and salt into a large bowl. Make a well in the middle of the flour mixture and pour in the liquid ingredients, stirring all the time. Use your hands to bring the mixture together to form a soft dough. Turn it out onto a well-floured work surface and knead for 10 minutes, until soft, smooth, and elastic.

2 Place the dough in a large, lightly oiled bowl, cover with plastic wrap, and leave to rise in a warm place for 1–2 hours, until doubled in size.

3 To make the filling, heat the butter and olive oil in a large, heavy saucepan. Put in the onions and caraway seeds, and season well with salt and pepper. Cook gently for about 20 minutes, covered, until they are soft but not brown. Remove the lid and cook for another 5 minutes until any excess water evaporates.

4 In a separate bowl, whisk together the sour cream, crème fraîche, eggs, and flour, and season well. Mix in the cooked onions and set aside to cool.

5 When the dough has risen well, turn it out onto a floured work surface and push it down gently with your knuckles to knock it back. Lightly oil the baking sheet. Roll the dough out to roughly the size of the sheet and line the sheet with it, making sure the pie has an upturned edge. Use your fingers to ease the dough into position, if necessary. Cover with lightly oiled plastic wrap and leave to rise in a warm place for another 30 minutes until puffy in places.

6 Preheat the oven to 400°F (200°C). Gently push down the dough if it has risen too much around the edges of the sheet. Spread the filling out over the pie base and sprinkle the top with bacon.

7 Place the baking sheet on the top rack of the oven and bake for 35–40 minutes until golden brown. Remove from the oven and leave to cool for at least 5 minutes before serving. Serve warm or cold.

PREPARE AHEAD Cover and chill overnight.

BAKER'S TIP

This delicious onion and sour cream tart looks like a cross between a pizza and a tart, and is indeed made with a traditional pizza dough base. It is not much known outside its native country, but is well worth making. It was traditionally served during grape harvesting time in parts of Germany.

Pita Bread

This pocket bread is delicious stuffed with salad and other fillings, or cut up and eaten with dips.

MAKES 6 PITAS — **20–30 MINS** — **5 MINS** — **UP TO 8 WEEKS**

Rising and proofing time
1 hr–1 hr 50 mins

Ingredients
1 tsp dried yeast
⅓ cup whole wheat flour
1⅓ cups bread flour, plus extra
   for dusting
1 tsp salt
2 tsp cumin seeds
2 tsp extra virgin olive oil, plus extra
   for greasing

1 In a small bowl, mix the yeast with ¾ cup lukewarm water. Leave 5 minutes, then stir.

2 In a large bowl, mix together the two types of flour, salt, and cumin seeds.

3 Make a well and pour in the dissolved yeast, ¾ cup lukewarm water, and oil.

4 Combine the flour mix with the wet ingredients, mixing to form a soft, sticky dough.

5 Turn the dough onto a floured work surface and knead until very smooth and elastic.

6 Place the dough in a lightly greased bowl and cover with a damp kitchen towel.

7 Leave to rise in a warm place for 1–1½ hours, until doubled in size. Flour 2 baking sheets.

8 Turn the dough onto a lightly floured work surface, and knock back.

9 Shape the dough into a cylinder 2in (5cm) wide, then cut into 6 pieces.

10 Take 1 piece of dough and leave the rest covered with a kitchen towel as you work.

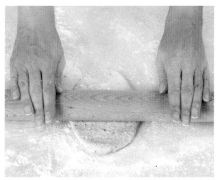

11 Shape the dough into a ball, then roll into an 8in (20cm) oval.

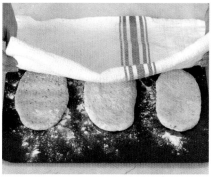

12 Transfer to a baking sheet. Repeat to shape the remaining pitas. Cover with a kitchen towel.

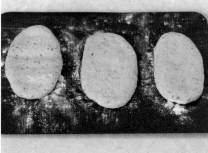

13 Leave to rise in a warm place for 20 minutes. Preheat the oven to 475°F (240°C).

14 Place another baking sheet in the oven. Once hot, transfer half the pitas to the sheet.

15 Bake for 5 minutes. Transfer to a wire rack and brush the tops lightly with water.

16 Bake the remaining rounds, transfer to the rack, and brush with water. **STORE** Best eaten warm from the oven, pitas can be stored overnight in an airtight container.

Pita variations

Spiced Lamb Pies

Snacks such as these are found all around the Middle East.

MAKES 12 PIES | 40–45 MINS | 10–15 MINS

Rising and proofing time
1 hr–1 hr 50 mins

Ingredients
1 quantity pita dough, see page 92,
  steps 1–8, omitting the cumin seeds
2 tbsp extra virgin olive oil
13oz (375g) ground lamb
sea salt
freshly ground black pepper
3 large garlic cloves, finely chopped
½in (1cm) piece of fresh ginger, finely chopped
1 onion, finely chopped
½ tsp ground coriander
¼ tsp ground cumin
¼ tsp ground turmeric
large pinch of cayenne pepper
2 tomatoes, peeled, seeded, and chopped
leaves from 5–7 cilantro sprigs, finely chopped

Method
1 Heat the oil in a sauté pan. Add the lamb, season with salt and pepper, and stir over medium-high heat, until evenly browned. With a slotted spoon, transfer to a bowl. Reduce the heat to medium, and pour off all but 2 tablespoons of the fat. Add the garlic and ginger and cook for 30 seconds. Add the onion and stir until soft. Add the ground coriander, cumin, turmeric, cayenne, lamb, and tomatoes. Cover and cook for 10 minutes, until thickened.

2 Remove the pan from the heat. Stir in the cilantro and taste for seasoning. Let the filling cool, then taste again: it should be well seasoned, so adjust if necessary.

3 Cut the dough in half. Shape 1 piece into a cylinder about 2in (5cm) in diameter. Cut into 6 pieces, and cover. Repeat with the remaining dough. Shape a piece of dough into a ball. With a rolling pin, roll into a 4in (10cm) round. Spoon some of the lamb into the center of the round, leaving a 1in (2.5cm) border. Lift the dough up and over the filling, to form a triangular parcel. Pinch

the edges with your fingers to seal. Place the pie on a baking sheet. Repeat to shape and fill the remaining dough.

4 Cover the pies with a kitchen towel, and let rise in a warm place until puffed, about 20 minutes. Preheat the oven to 450°F (230°C). Bake for 10–15 minutes until golden brown. Serve warm from the oven with a spoonful of Greek yogurt on the side, if you like.

STORE The pies will keep in an airtight container overnight.

PREPARE AHEAD The lamb filling can be prepared, covered, and refrigerated 1 day ahead.

Spiced Garbanzo Bean Pitas

These are good grilled, and best eaten on the day they are made.

MAKES 8 PITAS · **25 MINS** · **15 MINS**

Rising time
1 hr

Ingredients

1 tsp dried yeast
1½ tsp cumin seeds, plus more for sprinkling
1½ tsp ground coriander
3½ cups bread flour, plus extra for dusting
1 tsp salt
small bunch of cilantro, coarsely chopped
7oz (200g) can garbanzo beans, drained and crushed
⅔ cup plain yogurt
1 tbsp extra virgin olive oil, plus extra for greasing

Method

1 Sprinkle the yeast over 1¼ cups lukewarm water and allow to dissolve, stirring once. Toast the cumin and ground coriander in a dry pan for a minute. Mix the flour and salt in a bowl. Stir in the spices, cilantro, and garbanzo beans, then make a well in the middle. Pour in the yogurt, oil, and yeast liquid, and bring together to form a sticky dough. Set aside for 10 minutes.

2 Turn the dough out onto a floured surface, and knead it for 5 minutes, shaping it into a ball. Place the dough in an oiled bowl, cover it with oiled plastic wrap, and leave it to rise in a warm place for 1 hour, or until doubled in size.

3 Dust 2 baking sheets with flour. Preheat the oven to 425°F (220°C). Turn the dough out onto a floured surface. Cut into 8 pieces.

4 Using a rolling pin, flatten them out into ovals, each about ¼in (5mm) thick. Place them on the baking sheets, brush with oil, and scatter over cumin seeds. Bake for 15 minutes, or until golden and puffed up.

STORE The pitas will keep in an airtight container overnight.

Pita Chips

Serve these simple, homemade pita chips as part of a range of appetizers for a healthier alternative to potato chips.

SERVES 8 · **10 MINS** · **7–8 MINS**

Ingredients

6 pita breads, store-bought, or see pages 92–93
extra virgin olive oil, for greasing
cayenne pepper, for sprinkling
sea salt, for sprinkling

Method

1 Preheat the oven to 450°F (230°C). Divide the pita breads in half by separating the 2 layers of bread. Brush the pieces of bread on both sides with a little olive oil, then sprinkle them with salt and a scattering of cayenne pepper.

2 Stack the pieces of pita bread on top of each other in piles of 6, and cut them into large triangles. Lay the cut chips out onto several large baking sheets in a single layer, making sure they do not overlap.

3 Bake the chips in the top of the oven for 5 minutes, or until the bottoms are starting to brown. Turn over and continue to cook for another 2–3 minutes until they are browned and crisp all over. Watch them to make sure that they do not burn. Leave to cool on paper towels, and serve with dips such as baba ganoush or hummus.

STORE The chips will keep in an airtight container for 2 days.

PITA VARIATIONS

BAKER'S TIP

These simple snacks go well with homemade dips and salsas, or even chili con carne. They are an inexpensive alternative to chips, and much healthier too! To make them even more nutritious, bake whole wheat pita chips instead.

Naan Bread

This familiar Indian flat bread is traditionally cooked in a tandoor oven, but this recipe uses a conventional oven.

MAKES
6 NAAN

20
MINS

8
MINS

UP TO 12
WEEKS

Rising time
1 hr

Ingredients

2¾ cups bread flour, plus extra for
  dusting
2 tsp dried yeast
1 tsp sugar
1 tsp salt
2 tsp black onion seeds
½ cup full-fat plain yogurt
4 tbsp ghee, or butter, melted

1 Heat the ghee or butter in a small saucepan until melted. Set aside.

2 In a large bowl, mix together the flour, yeast, sugar, salt, and onion seeds.

3 Make a well. Add ¾ cup lukewarm water, the yogurt, and the melted ghee.

4 Draw in the flour and mix gently with a wooden spoon to combine.

5 Keep mixing for 5 minutes, until it forms a rough dough.

6 Cover and keep warm until doubled, about 1 hour. Preheat the oven to 475°F (240°C).

7 Place 2 baking sheets in the oven. Knock back the dough.

8 Knead the dough on a floured surface until smooth. Divide into 4 equal pieces.

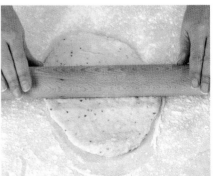

9 Roll each piece into an oval shape about 10in (24cm) long.

10 Transfer the bread to preheated sheets and bake for 6–7 minutes, until well puffed.

11 Preheat the broiler to its hottest setting. Transfer the breads to the broiler pan.

12 Cook the naans for 30–40 seconds on each side, or until they brown and blister.

13 When broiling, be sure not to put the breads too close to the heat, to prevent burning. Transfer to a wire rack and serve warm.

ALSO TRY... Garlic and Cilantro Naan Add 2 crushed garlic cloves and 4 tablespoons finely chopped cilantro in step 2.

Naan variations

Feta, Chile, and Herb-stuffed Naan

Try stuffing a simple naan bread dough with this herby feta mix for an unusual picnic dish, which brings together flavors of the Mediterranean with those of India.

**MAKES
6 NAAN** **15
MINS** **6–7
MINS**

Rising time
1 hr

Ingredients
1 quantity naan bread dough, see page 96, steps 1–7
6oz (150g) feta cheese, crumbled
1 tbsp finely chopped red or jalapeño chile
3 tbsp chopped mint
3 tbsp chopped cilantro

Method

1 Make the naan dough up to the end of step 7 (see page 96). Make the stuffing by mixing together the feta, chile, and herbs. Preheat the oven to 475°F (240°C) and place 2 large baking sheets in the oven.

2 Divide the dough into 6, and roll each piece into a circle. Divide the filling into 6, and put 1 portion of the filling into the middle of each piece of dough. Pull the edges up around it to form a purse shape. Pinch the edges together to seal.

3 Turn the dough over and roll out carefully into an oval, making sure not to tear the dough or reveal any of the filling.

4 Carefully transfer the breads onto the preheated baking sheets and cook in

the oven for 6–7 minutes, or until well puffed. Carefully transfer to a wire rack, and serve while still warm.

PREPARE AHEAD These can be stored overnight, wrapped in plastic wrap. To reheat (from fresh or frozen), scrunch up a piece of parchment paper and soak in water. Squeeze out the excess water, and use to wrap the naan. Place in a warm oven for 10 minutes until warm and soft.

Peshwari Naan

Children love these sweet, nutty stuffed naans, best eaten still warm from the pan, either as a dessert or a side dish to savory curry. Try substituting finely chopped apple for the raisins and adding some cinnamon. ▶

**MAKES
6 NAAN** **15
MINS** **6–7
MINS** **UP TO 8
WEEKS**

Rising time
1 hr

Special equipment
food processor with blade attachment

Ingredients
1 quantity naan bread dough, see page 96, steps 1–7
2 tbsp raisins
2 tbsp unsalted pistachios
2 tbsp almonds
2 tbsp unsweetened coconut
1 tbsp sugar

Method

1 Make the naan dough up to the end of step 7 (see page 96). Make the stuffing by putting all the remaining ingredients in a food processor, and purée until finely chopped. Preheat the oven to 475°F (240°C) and place 2 large baking sheets in the oven.

2 Divide the dough into 6, and roll each piece into a circle. Divide the filling into 6. Put 1 portion of the filling into the middle of each piece of dough, and pull the edges up around it to form a purse shape. Pinch the edges together to seal.

3 Turn the dough over and roll out carefully into an oval, making sure not to tear the dough or reveal any of the filling.

4 Carefully transfer the breads onto the preheated baking sheets and cook in the oven for 6–7 minutes, or until well puffed. Carefully transfer to a wire rack, and serve while still warm.

PREPARE AHEAD These can be stored overnight, wrapped in plastic wrap. To reheat (from fresh or frozen), scrunch up a piece of parchment paper and soak in water. Squeeze out the excess water, and use to wrap the peshwari naan. Place them in a warm oven for 10 minutes until they are warm and soft.

BAKER'S TIP
Once you have mastered the art of stuffing naan dough, there's no end to the things you can fill it with. Here the naan is stuffed with a mixture of nuts and dried fruit, sweetened with shredded coconut. Try a spiced lamb filling as well, and serve with a minted yogurt dip.

Stuffed Paratha

These stuffed flat breads are quick and easy to make. Try doubling the quantities, then freezing half stacked between layers of wax paper.

| MAKES 4 | 20 MINS | 15–20 MINS | UP TO 8 WEEKS |

Rising time
1 hr

Ingredients

For the dough
1½ cups chapatti flour
½ tsp fine salt
4 tbsp unsalted butter, melted and cooled

For the stuffing
9oz (250g) sweet potato, peeled and diced
1 tbsp sunflower or vegetable oil, plus extra
  for brushing
½ red onion, finely chopped
2 garlic cloves, crushed
1 tbsp finely chopped red or jalapeño chile,
  or to taste
1 tbsp finely chopped fresh ginger
2 heaping tbsp chopped cilantro
½ tsp garam masala
sea salt

Method

1 To make the dough, sift the flour and salt together. Add the butter and ⅔ cup water and bring the mixture together to form a soft dough. Knead by hand for 10 minutes, or for 5 minutes in the electric mixer, then leave the dough to rest, covered, for 1 hour.

2 Boil the sweet potato for about 7 minutes, until tender. Drain well. In a frying pan, heat the sunflower oil over medium heat, and cook the red onion for 3–5 minutes, until soft, but not golden. Add the garlic, chile, and ginger and cook for 1–2 minutes.

3 Add the cooked onion mixture to the sweet potato and mash. You should not need any extra liquid. Add the chopped cilantro, garam masala, and salt and beat until smooth. Set aside to cool.

4 When the dough has rested, divide it into 4 equal pieces. Knead each piece a little and roll it out into a small circle, around 4in (10cm) in diameter. Put a quarter of the stuffing mixture into the middle of the dough and pull the edges up around it into the middle, forming a purse shape.

5 Pinch the edges together to seal in the stuffing, turn the dough over, and roll out carefully into a circle about 7in (18cm) in diameter, making sure not to roll too hard. If the filling bursts out of the dough, pinch the dough together to reseal the paratha.

6 Heat a large cast iron frying pan over medium heat. Cook the parathas for 2 minutes on each side, turning occasionally to make sure they are well cooked and browning in places. Once they have cooked on each side once, brush the surface with a little sunflower oil before turning them again. Serve immediately alongside a curry, or as a light lunch dish with a green salad.

PREPARE AHEAD These can be stored overnight, wrapped in plastic wrap. To reheat (from fresh or frozen), scrunch up a piece of parchment paper and soak in water. Squeeze out the excess water, and use to wrap the parathas. Place them in a warm oven for 10 minutes until soft.

BAKER'S TIP

These Indian flat breads are made with traditional chapatti flour, but if you cannot find it easily, use whole wheat flour instead. Try stuffing them with a variety of fillings, including leftover vegetable curry; just make sure the ingredients are diced small so the stuffing is easily contained.

Tortillas

These classic Mexican flat breads are simple to make and far tastier than any store-bought tortilla.

MAKES 8 | 10 MINS | 15–20 MINS | UP TO 8 WEEKS

Resting time
1 hr

Ingredients

1¾ cups all-purpose flour, plus extra
  for dusting
scant 1 tsp salt
½ tsp baking powder
4 tbsp lard or vegetable shortening,
  chilled and diced, plus extra
  for greasing

1 Put the flour, salt, and baking powder into a large bowl. Add the lard.

2 Rub the lard in with your hands until the mixture resembles fine crumbs.

3 Add ⅔ cup warm water. Bring the mixture together to form a rough, soft dough.

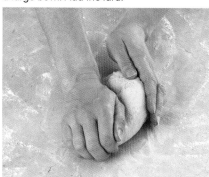

4 Turn it out onto a lightly floured work surface and knead for a few minutes until smooth.

5 Put the dough in a greased bowl. Cover with plastic wrap. Rest in a warm place for 1 hour.

6 Turn the dough out onto a floured work surface and divide it into 8 equal portions.

7 Take 1 piece and leave the others covered with plastic wrap to prevent them from drying.

8 Roll each piece of dough out thinly to a circle about 8–10in (20–25cm) in diameter.

9 Stack the rolled tortillas in a pile. Place a piece of parchment paper between each.

10 Heat a pan over medium heat. Take 1 tortilla and dry fry for 1 minute.

11 Turn it over and continue to cook until both sides are cooked and browned in places.

12 Transfer to a wire rack and repeat to cook all the remaining tortillas. Serve warm or cool.

PREPARE AHEAD Cooled tortillas can be stored overnight, wrapped in plastic wrap. To reheat from fresh or frozen, scrunch up wax paper and soak it in water. Squeeze out the excess, use to wrap the tortillas, and bake in a medium oven for 10 minutes.

Tortilla variations

Quesadillas

Almost any filling works for quesadillas: try substituting chicken, ham, Gruyère cheese, or mushrooms.

MAKES 1 OF EACH | 5–10 MINS | 30–35 MINS

Ingredients

For the spiced beef and tomato filling
1 tbsp extra virgin olive oil
6oz (150g) good-quality ground beef
pinch of hot cayenne pepper
sea salt
freshly ground black pepper
small handful fresh flat-leaf parsley, chopped
2 tomatoes, diced
2oz (50g) Cheddar cheese

For the avocado, scallion, and chile filling
4 scallions, finely chopped
1–2 fresh jalapeño chiles, seeded and chopped
juice of ½ lime
½ avocado, sliced
2oz (50g) Cheddar cheese

For the tortillas
2 tbsp oil
4 tortillas, see pages 102–103

Method

1 For the beef filling, heat 1 tablespoon of the oil in a frying pan, then cook the beef with the cayenne pepper over medium heat for 5 minutes, or until no longer pink. Reduce the heat and loosen with a little hot water. Season, and cook for 10 minutes, until the beef is cooked through. Stir in the parsley.

2 For the avocado filling, place the scallion, chiles, and lime juice in a bowl. Season and mix. Set aside for 2 minutes.

3 Heat half the oil for the tortillas in a non-stick frying pan. Cook 1 tortilla for 1 minute, or until lightly golden. Spoon the beef mixture over. Scatter over the tomato and cheese, then top with the other tortilla, pressing it down with the back of a spatula to sandwich the two. Scoop the quesadilla up, carefully turn it over, and cook the other side for another minute, or until golden. Slice in halves or quarters, and serve.

4 Heat the remaining oil in the frying pan, then cook 1 tortilla for 1 minute, or until golden. Scatter over the avocado, leaving a little space around the edge, spoon on the scallion mixture, and sprinkle with the cheese. Continue as in step 3.

Kids' Hot Tortilla Sandwiches

A quick alternative to a sandwich lunch that kids love.

SERVES 2 | 10 MINS | 8 MINS

Ingredients

4 tortillas, store-bought, or see pages 102–103
4 thin slices ham
ketchup, mild mustard, or chili sauce
2oz (50g) grated cheese, such as Cheddar
carrots, peeled and chopped, to serve (optional)
cucumber, chopped, to serve (optional)

Method

1 Place 2 of the tortillas on the work surface. Place 2 slices of ham on each tortilla, trying to ensure that the ham covers the whole tortilla. Tear it a little and spread it out if necessary.

2 Depending on your children's tastes, you could spread a little ketchup, mild mustard, or chili sauce over the top of the ham. Sprinkle the grated cheese evenly over both the tortillas, and top with a second tortilla to make a sandwich.

3 Heat a large frying pan (big enough to take the tortillas) over medium heat. Cook the tortillas 1 at a time for 1 minute on each side. Turn them after each minute and continue to cook until both sides are cooked and browned in places.

4 Cut each tortilla into 8 segments, as you would a pizza, and serve immediately, with some chopped carrot and cucumber for a quick lunch.

FLAT BREADS AND CRISP BREADS

Prawn and Guacamole Tortilla Stacks

These sophisticated Mexican-style canapés are simple to make.

MAKES 50 | 15 MINS | 5 MINS

Special equipment
1¼in (3cm) pastry cutter
piping bag with small plain nozzle

Ingredients
5 tortillas, store-bought, or see pages 102–103
1.5 quarts (1.5 liters) sunflower or vegetable oil, for deep-frying
2 ripe avocados
1 lime
Tabasco sauce
¼ cup finely chopped cilantro
4 scallions, trimmed and finely chopped
sea salt
freshly ground black pepper
25 cooked king prawns, peeled and deveined

Method

1 Cut 100 disks out of the tortillas with the pastry cutter. Heat the oil in a large saucepan. Drop the tortillas into the oil a handful at a time and deep-fry until golden. Do not overcrowd the pan, or the tortillas will not crisp properly. Remove and drain on paper towels. Cool.

2 Mash the avocado with the juice of half the lime, a few shakes of Tabasco, 3 tablespoons cilantro, the scallion, and salt and pepper to taste. Slice each prawn in half horizontally.

3 When there are 30 minutes left before serving, marinate the prawns with the juice of the other half of the lime and the remainder of the chopped cilantro.

4 Pipe a little guacamole on a tortilla, top it with another tortilla, pipe more guacamole on top, and finish with a curl of prawn. If it is too big, twist diagonally and stand it up in the guacamole. Serve immediately.

PREPARE AHEAD The fried tortilla disks can be stored in an airtight container for 2 days.

Sesame Grissini

Tradition has it that breadsticks should be pulled the length of the baker's arm—these are more manageable!

MAKES 32 **40–45 MINS** **15–18 MINS**

Rising time
1–1½ hrs

Ingredients
2½ tsp dried yeast
2¼ cups bread flour,
  plus extra for dusting
1 tbsp sugar
2 tsp salt
2 tbsp extra virgin olive oil, plus
  extra for glazing and greasing
½ cup sesame seeds

FLAT BREADS AND CRISP BREADS

1 Sprinkle the yeast over ¼ cup lukewarm water. Leave for 5 minutes, stirring once.

2 Put the flour, sugar, and salt in a bowl. Add the yeast and 1 cup more lukewarm water.

3 Add the oil and draw the flour into the liquid, mixing to form a soft, slightly sticky dough.

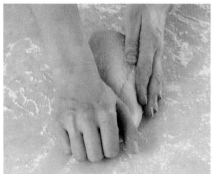  

4 Knead the dough on a floured surface for 5–7 minutes, until very smooth and elastic.

5 Cover the dough with a damp kitchen towel and let it rest for about 5 minutes.

6 Flour your hands and pat the dough into a rectangle on a well-floured work surface.

7 Roll the dough out to a 16 x 6in (40 x 15cm) rectangle. Cover it with a damp kitchen towel.

8 Leave in a warm place for 1–1½ hours until doubled. Preheat oven to 425°F (220°C).

9 Dust 3 baking sheets with flour. Brush the dough with water. Sprinkle with sesame seeds.

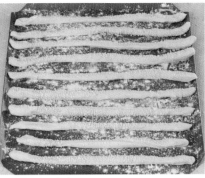

10 With a sharp knife, cut the dough into 32 strips, each about ½in (1cm) wide.

11 Stretch 1 strip to the width of a baking sheet. Set it on 1 of the prepared baking sheets.

12 Repeat with the remaining strips, arranging them ¾in (2cm) apart.

13 Bake for 15–18 minutes, until golden and crisp. Transfer to a wire rack and let cool completely.
STORE These will keep in an airtight container for 2 days.

Grissini variations

Spanish Picos

These miniature Spanish breadsticks are made by tying strips of dough in loops and are a great addition to a tapas meal.

MAKES 16 · **40–45 MINS** · **18–20 MINS**

Rising time
1–1½ hrs

Ingredients
½ quantity grissini dough, see page 106, steps 1–6
1½ tbsp sea salt

Method
1 Roll out the dough to an 8 x 6in (20 x 15cm) rectangle. Cover with a damp kitchen towel and leave to rise in a warm place for 1–1½ hours until doubled in size.

2 Preheat the oven to 425°F (220°C). Dust 2 baking sheets with flour. Cut the dough into 16 strips, then cut each strip into half. Take a half strip, loop it, twist the ends in a single knot, and transfer to a prepared baking sheet. Repeat to shape the remaining strips.

3 Lightly brush the loops with water and sprinkle with the sea salt. Bake the loops for 18–20 minutes, until golden and crisp. Let cool as directed.

STORE The picos can be kept for 2 days in an airtight container.

Parmesan Grissini

Smoked paprika adds a depth of flavor to these cheesy grissini.

MAKES 32 · **40–45 MINS** · **10 MINS**

Rising time
1–1½ hrs

Ingredients
2½ tsp dried yeast
2¼ cups all-purpose flour, plus extra for dusting
1 tbsp sugar
2 tsp salt
1½ tsp smoked paprika
2 tbsp olive oil, extra for glazing and greasing
2oz (50g) Parmesan cheese, grated

Method
1 Sprinkle the yeast over ¼ cup lukewarm water. Leave for 5 minutes until dissolved, stirring once. Put the flour, sugar, salt, and smoked paprika in a bowl. Pour in the oil, dissolved yeast, and 1 cup more lukewarm water.

2 Draw in the flour to form a dough; it should be soft and sticky. Flour the surface and knead for 5–7 minutes, until it is smooth and forms a ball. Cover with a damp kitchen towel and leave for 5 minutes. Flour your hands and pat the dough into a rectangle on a floured surface. Roll it out to a 16 x 6in (40 x 15cm) rectangle. Cover with the kitchen towel and leave for 1–1½ hours, until doubled in size.

3 Preheat the oven to 425°F (220°C). Dust 3 baking sheets with flour and lightly brush the dough with water. Sprinkle with Parmesan, pressing it down gently. With a sharp knife, cut the dough into 32 strips, each ½in (1cm) wide. Stretch 1 strip to the width of a baking sheet, and set on 1 of the prepared sheets. Repeat with the remaining strips, placing them ¾in (2cm) apart. Bake for 10 minutes, until golden and crisp. Transfer to a wire rack to cool.

STORE Best eaten fresh, these will keep in an airtight container for 2 days.

Prosciutto-wrapped Canapés

Try dipping these quick homemade canapés in herb mayo or salsa verde.

MAKES 32 | 45 MINS | 15–18 MINS

Rising time
1–1½ hrs

Ingredients
1 quantity grissini dough,
 see page 106, steps 1–8
3 tbsp sea salt
12 slices prosciutto

Method

1 Preheat the oven to 425°F (220°C) and dust 3 baking sheets with flour. Brush the rolled out dough with water and sprinkle with sea salt crystals.

2 With a sharp knife, cut the dough into 32 strips, each ½in (1cm) wide. Stretch each one to the width of the baking sheet and position ¾in (2cm) apart. Bake for 15–18 minutes, until golden and crisp. Cool on a wire rack.

3 Cut each slice of prosciutto lengthwise into 3. Wrap each grissini at one end with one-third of a slice of ham just before serving as a canapé.

PREPARE AHEAD The grissini can be made 1 day ahead and stored unwrapped in an airtight container.

BAKER'S TIP

Homemade grissini are a lovely addition to a party menu. Experiment by adding flavor and texture, using things such as chopped olives, or smoked paprika, or your favorite cheeses; or leave them plain for a healthy and child-friendly snack. They will be at their best if eaten on the day they are baked.

Stilton and Walnut Biscuits

These savory biscuits are an ideal way to use up the leftover cheese and nuts you usually have after Christmas.

MAKES 24 | 10 MINS | 20 MINS | 12 WEEKS, UNBAKED

Chilling time
1 hr

Special equipment
2in (5cm) round pastry cutter

Ingredients
5oz (120g) Stilton cheese, or other blue cheese
4 tbsp unsalted butter, softened
¾ cup all-purpose flour, sifted, plus extra for dusting
⅓ cup walnuts, chopped
freshly ground black pepper
1 large egg yolk, at room temperature

1 Mix together the cheese and butter with an electric hand mixer until soft and creamy.

2 Add the flour to the cheese mixture and rub in with your fingertips to form bread crumbs.

3 Add the walnuts and black pepper and stir to mix through.

4 Finally add the egg yolk and bring the mixture together to form a stiff dough.

5 Knead the dough briefly on a lightly floured work surface to help blend in the walnuts.

6 Wrap the dough in plastic wrap. Chill for 1 hour. Preheat the oven to 350°F (180°C).

7 Turn the dough out onto a floured work surface and knead briefly to soften slightly.

8 Roll it out to a thickness of ¼in (5mm) and cut out the biscuits with the pastry cutter.

9 Alternatively, the dough can be chilled as an even 2in (5cm) diameter log.

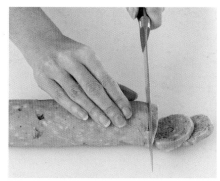 

10 Slice the dough log carefully into ¼in (5mm) rounds with a sharp knife.

11 Put the rounds on non-stick baking sheets and bake in the top of the oven for 15 minutes.

12 Turn them over and bake for another 5 minutes until golden brown on both sides.

13 Remove from the oven, allow to cool a little on their sheets, then transfer to a wire rack to cool completely.

STORE The biscuits will keep in an airtight container for 5 days.

Cheese Biscuit variations

Parmesan and Rosemary Thins

These savory crackers are light and elegant, and are equally good served as an appetizer before a meal or after dinner with cheese.

MAKES 15–20 | **10 MINS** | **15 MINS** | **12 WEEKS, UNBAKED**

Chilling time
1 hr

Special equipment
2½in (6cm) round cookie cutter
food processor with blade attachment (optional)

Ingredients
4 tbsp unsalted butter, softened and diced
½ cup all-purpose flour, plus extra for dusting
2oz (60g) Parmesan cheese, finely grated
freshly grated black pepper
1 tbsp chopped rosemary, thyme, or basil

Method

1 Place the butter and flour in a bowl, or in the bowl of a food processor. Rub together with your fingertips or pulse-blend until the mixture resembles crumbs. Add the Parmesan, black pepper, and chopped herbs and mix in thoroughly. Bring the mixture together to form a dough.

2 Turn the dough out on to a lightly floured work surface and knead briefly to help it amalgamate, then wrap it in plastic wrap and chill for 1 hour.

3 Preheat the oven to 350°F (180°C). Turn the dough out on to a lightly floured work surface and knead briefly to soften slightly.

4 Roll the dough out to ½in (2mm) thick and cut out the thins with the cookie cutter. Place on 2 non-stick baking sheets and bake in the top of the oven for 10 minutes, then turn them over and continue to bake for 5 minutes, until lightly browned.

5 Remove from the oven and allow to cool on the sheets for 5 minutes before transferring to a wire rack to cool.

STORE The thins will keep in an airtight container for 3 days.

Cheese Thins

These spicy crackers can be made in bulk for an easy party snack.

MAKES 30 | **10 MINS** | **15 MINS** | **8 WEEKS, UNBAKED**

Chilling time
1 hr

Special equipment
2½in (6cm) round pastry cutter
food processor with blade attachment (optional)

Ingredients
4 tbsp unsalted butter, softened and diced
¾ cup all-purpose flour, plus extra for dusting
6oz (150g) strong Cheddar cheese, finely grated
½ tsp smoked paprika or cayenne pepper
1 large egg yolk, at room temperature

Method

1 Place the butter and flour in a bowl, or in the bowl of a food processor with a blade attachment. Rub together or pulse-blend until the mixture resembles crumbs. Add the Cheddar and the smoked paprika and mix thoroughly. Add the egg yolk and bring the mixture together to form a dough.

2 Turn the dough out on to a lightly floured work surface and knead it briefly to help it amalgamate, then wrap it in plastic wrap and chill for 1 hour. When ready to bake, preheat the oven to 350°F (180°C). Turn the dough out and knead briefly to soften.

3 Roll the dough out to a thickness of ½in (2mm) and cut out the thins with the cookie cutter. Place them onto several non-stick baking sheets and bake at the top of the oven for 10 minutes, then turn them over, pressing down gently with a spatula to flatten any air bubbles that appear. Continue to bake for another 5 minutes, until golden brown on both sides.

4 Remove from the oven and leave them on the sheets for 5 minutes before transferring to a wire rack to cool completely.

STORE The thins will keep in an airtight container for 3 days.

Cheese Straws

A great way to use up any leftover pieces of hard cheese.

| MAKES 15–20 | 10 MINS | 15 MINS | 12 WEEKS, UNBAKED |

Chilling time
1 hr

Special equipment
food processor with blade attachment (optional)

Ingredients
½ cup flour, sifted, plus extra for dusting
pinch of salt
4 tbsp unsalted butter, softened and diced
1oz (30g) strong Cheddar cheese, finely grated
1 large egg yolk, plus 1 egg extra,
   beaten, for glazing
1 tsp Dijon mustard

Method

1 Place the flour, salt, and butter in a bowl, or the bowl of a food processor. Rub together with your fingertips or pulse-blend until the mixture resembles crumbs. Add the Cheddar and mix in. Whisk the egg yolk with 1 tablespoon cold water and the mustard until combined. Add to the crumbs and bring it together to form a dough.

2 Turn the dough out onto a lightly floured work surface and knead briefly. Wrap it in plastic wrap and chill for 1 hour. Preheat the oven to 400°F (200°C). When ready to cook, briefly knead the dough again.

3 Roll the dough out to a 12 x 6in (30 x 15cm) rectangle; it should be ¼in (5mm) thick. With a sharp knife, cut ½in (1cm) wide lengths along the shorter side. Brush the strips of pastry with a little beaten egg. Holding the top of each strip, twist the bottom of the strip gently a few times to form spirals.

4 Place the straws on non-stick baking sheets, pressing down the ends if the spirals appear to be unwinding. Bake in the top of the oven for 15 minutes. Cool on the sheets for 5 minutes, then transfer to a wire rack.

STORE The straws will keep in an airtight container for 3 days.

Oatcakes

These Scottish oatcakes are perfect with cheese and chutney. Made with just oats (see Baker's Tip), they become a good wheat-free option.

MAKES 16	20 MINS	15 MINS	UP TO 4 WEEKS

¾ tsp salt
freshly ground black pepper
½ tsp baking soda
2 tbsp olive oil

Special equipment
2½in (6cm) round cookie cutter

Ingredients
1¼ cups rolled oats, plus extra for dusting
¾ cup whole wheat flour, plus extra for dusting

Method

1 Preheat the oven to 350°F (180°C). Mix the dry ingredients together in a bowl. Whisk together the oil with 4 tablespoons freshly boiled water. Make a well in the center of the flour mixture and pour in the liquid, mixing it together with a spoon to form a thick paste.

2 Lightly flour a work surface with a mixture of flour and oats and turn the paste out onto it. Knead together briefly until it forms a dough. Gently roll the dough out, being aware that the more oats you use, the more delicate it will be and cracking is likely.

3 It is difficult to bring the pastry together again after the first rolling, so cut as many oatcakes as possible with the first rolling. Roll the dough to a thickness of ¼in (5mm) and cut out the oatcakes. If the dough has difficulty coming together after the first cutting, put it back in the bowl and add a drop or two of water to help it amalgamate again, then re-roll and cut more oatcakes.

4 Place the oatcakes on several non-stick baking sheets and bake at the top of the oven for 10 minutes, then turn them over and continue to bake for another 5 minutes, until golden brown on both sides. Remove the oatcakes from the oven and leave on the sheets for 5 minutes, before transferring to a wire rack to cool completely.

STORE The oatcakes will keep in an airtight container for 3 days.

BAKER'S TIP

These traditional Scottish oatcakes can be made using just oats, or with a mixture of both oats and whole wheat flour. Made using only oats they are ideal for those who want to avoid wheat, but this does produce a more delicate, crumbly cake, and will need gentle handling when cutting out.

FLAT BREADS AND CRISP BREADS

quick breads & batters

Soda Bread

This has a light, cakelike texture. As an added bonus, it requires no kneading, so is a wonderfully effort-free loaf.

MAKES 1 LOAF **10–15 MINS** **35–40 MINS**

Ingredients

unsalted butter, for greasing
3 cups whole wheat flour,
   plus extra for dusting
1½ tsp baking soda
1½ tsp salt
2 cups buttermilk,
   plus extra if needed

1 Preheat the oven to 400°F (200°C). Grease a baking sheet with butter.

2 Sift the flour, baking soda, and salt into a large bowl, adding in any leftover bran.

3 Mix thoroughly to combine and make a well in the center.

4 Gradually pour the buttermilk into the center of the well.

5 With your hands, quickly draw in the flour to make a soft, slightly sticky dough.

6 Do not overwork the dough. Add a little more buttermilk if it seems dry.

7 Turn the dough out onto a floured surface, and quickly shape into a round loaf.

8 Put the loaf on the baking sheet and pat it down into a round, about 2in (5cm) high.

9 Make a cross ½in (1cm) deep in the top of the loaf with a very sharp knife or scalpel.

10 Bake the loaf in the preheated oven for 35–40 minutes, until brown.

11 Turn the loaf over and tap the bottom. The bread should sound hollow.

12 Transfer the bread to a wire rack and let it cool slightly.

13 Cut the bread into slices or wedges and serve warm, with plenty of butter. Soda bread also makes very good toast.
STORE This will keep, well wrapped in paper, for 2–3 days.

NO!

Soda Bread variations

Skillet Bread

In this version, the dough is cut in wedges and cooked in a heavy frying pan or skillet, and the addition of white flour makes it a little lighter.

MAKES 4 WEDGES | **5–10 MINS** | **30–40 MINS**

Special equipment
lidded cast-iron frying pan

Ingredients
2⅓ cups stone-ground whole wheat flour
¾ cup bread flour,
   plus extra for dusting
1½ tsp baking soda
1 tsp salt
1⅔ cups buttermilk
unsalted butter, melted,
   for greasing

Method
1 Put the 2 types of flour, the baking soda, and salt into a large bowl, and make a well in the center. Pour the buttermilk into the well. With your hand, quickly draw the flour into the buttermilk to make a soft dough. It should be slightly sticky.

2 Turn the dough onto a lightly floured work surface, and quickly shape it into a round loaf. Pat the dough with the palms of your hands to form a round, about 2in (5cm) high. With a chef's knife, cut the round into 4 wedges.

3 Heat a large cast-iron frying pan to medium-low. Brush the heated pan with melted butter. Put the dough into the pan, cover, and cook, turning the wedges frequently, for 15–20 minutes, until golden brown, puffed, and cooked through. Serve warm, spread with soft cheese or butter.

Griddle Cakes

These sweet cakes are crisp on the outside and moist in the center.

MAKES 20 CAKES | **5–10 MINS** | **10 MINS**

Special equipment
griddle or large cast-iron frying pan

Ingredients
1⅓ cups stone-ground whole wheat flour
1½ tsp baking soda
1½ tsp salt
1 cup rolled oats
3 tbsp brown sugar
2 cups buttermilk
unsalted butter, melted, for greasing

Method
1 Put the flour, baking soda, and salt into a large bowl. Stir in the oats and sugar, and make a well in the center. Pour the buttermilk into the well. Stir, gradually drawing in the dry ingredients to make a smooth batter.

2 Heat a griddle or a large cast-iron frying pan to medium-low. Brush the heated griddle with melted butter. Using a small ladle, drop about 2 tablespoons batter onto the hot surface. Repeat to make 5–6 cakes. Cook for about 5 minutes, until the undersides of the griddle cakes are golden brown and crisp. Turn and brown them on the other side for about 5 minutes longer.

3 Transfer to a platter, cover, and keep warm. Continue with the remaining batter, brushing the griddle with more butter as needed. Serve the cakes warm with plenty of butter and jam.

American Soda Bread

This classic sweet bread can be ready for an afternoon snack in no time.

MAKES 1 LOAF | 10–15 MINS | 50–55 MINS | UP TO 8 WEEKS

Ingredients

2¼ cups all-purpose flour, plus extra for dusting
1 tsp fine salt
2 tsp baking powder
¼ cup sugar
1 tsp caraway seeds (optional)
4 tbsp unsalted butter, chilled and diced
⅔ cup raisins
1 large egg
⅔ cup buttermilk

Method

1 Preheat the oven to 350°F (180°C). In a large bowl mix together the flour, salt, baking powder, sugar, and caraway seeds (if using). Rub in the butter until the mixture resembles fine crumbs. Add the raisins and mix well to combine.

2 Whisk together the egg and the buttermilk. Make a well in the center of the flour mixture and gradually pour in the buttermilk mixture, stirring until it is all incorporated. You will need to use your hands at the end to bring it all together to form a loose, soft dough.

3 Turn the dough out onto a lightly floured work surface and knead it briefly until smooth. Shape it into a round about 6in (15cm) in diameter, and slash the top with a cross to allow the bread to rise easily.

4 Place the dough onto a baking sheet lined with parchment paper and cook in the middle of the preheated oven for 50–55 minutes, until well risen and golden brown. Transfer to a wire rack and allow to cool for at least 10 minutes before serving.

STORE This bread is best eaten the day it is baked, but will keep, well wrapped in paper, for 2 days.

Pumpkin Soda Bread

The use of grated pumpkin ensures this quick bread keeps moist for days. A perfect accompaniment for soup.

MAKES 1 LOAF	20 MINS	50 MINS	UP TO 8 WEEKS

Ingredients
1¾ cups all-purpose flour,
   plus extra for dusting
¾ cup whole wheat flour
1 tsp baking soda
½ tsp fine salt
⅓ cup pumpkin seeds
5oz (120g) pumpkin or butternut
   squash, coarsely grated
1¼ cups buttermilk

1 Preheat the oven to 425°F (220°C). In a large bowl, mix the flour, baking soda, and salt.

2 Add the grated pumpkin and seeds and stir well to combine so that no clumps remain.

3 Make a well in the center and pour in the buttermilk. Stir together to form a loose dough.

4 Use your hands to bring the mixture together into a ball, then turn out onto a floured surface.

5 Knead the dough for 2 minutes until it forms a smooth mass. You may need to add flour.

6 Shape the dough into a round 6in (15cm) in diameter. Place on a lined baking sheet.

7 Use a sharp knife to slash a cross into the top. This helps the bread to rise when baking.

8 Cook in the middle of the oven for 30 minutes, until risen. Reduce to 400°F (200°C).

9 Cook for another 20 minutes. The base should sound hollow when tapped.

10 Transfer the bread to a wire rack and allow it to cool for at least 20 minutes before serving. Cut the bread into wedges or slices, and serve as an accompaniment to soups and stews. **STORE** This will keep, well wrapped in paper, for 3 days.

Vegetable Soda Bread variations

Sweet Potato and Rosemary Rolls

The gentle scent of rosemary makes these rolls something special.

| MAKES 8 ROLLS | 20 MINS | 20–25 MINS | UP TO 8 WEEKS |

Ingredients

1½ cups all-purpose flour, plus extra for dusting
¾ cup whole wheat flour
1 tsp baking soda
½ tsp fine salt
freshly ground black pepper
5oz (140g) sweet potato
1 tsp finely chopped rosemary
1 cup buttermilk

Method

1 Preheat the oven to 425°F (220°C). Line a baking sheet with parchment paper. In a bowl mix the all-purpose flour, whole wheat flour, baking soda, salt, and pepper. Peel and coarsely grate the sweet potato, then chop it coarsely to reduce the size of the shreds. Add it to the bowl with the rosemary, mixing well so that no clumps form.

2 Make a well in the center of the dry ingredients and gently stir in the buttermilk, bringing the mixture together to form a loose dough. Use your hands to bring the mixture together into a ball, then turn it out onto a floured surface and knead for 2 minutes until it forms a smooth dough. You may need to add a little flour at this stage.

3 Divide the dough into 8 equal pieces and shape into tight rounds. Flatten the tops and cut a cross in the center of each roll to allow the dough to rise easily in the oven.

4 Place the rolls onto a baking sheet lined with parchment paper and cook them in the middle of the oven for 20-25 minutes, until well risen. Transfer to a wire rack and let cool for 10 minutes before serving. These are especially delicious eaten while warm.

STORE These rolls will keep, well wrapped in paper, for 3 days.

Zucchini and Hazelnut Bread

Hazelnuts add taste and texture to this quick and easy bread.

| MAKES 1 LOAF | 20 MINS | 50 MINS | UP TO 8 WEEKS |

Ingredients

1½ cups all-purpose flour, plus extra for dusting
1 cup whole wheat flour
1 tsp baking soda
½ tsp fine salt
⅓ cup hazelnuts, coarsely chopped
6oz (150g) zucchini
1 cup buttermilk

Method

1 Preheat the oven to 425°F (220°C). Mix together the all-purpose flour, whole wheat flour, baking soda, salt, and hazelnuts. Coarsely grate the zucchini and add it to the bowl, mixing well so that no clumps form.

2 Make a well in the center of the dry ingredients and stir in the buttermilk to form a loose, ragged dough. Use your hands to bring the mixture together into a ball, then turn it out onto a lightly floured work surface and knead for 2 minutes until it forms a smooth dough. You may need to add a little extra flour at this stage, depending on the water content of your vegetables.

3 Shape the dough into a round about 6in (15cm) in diameter, and slash the top with a cross to allow the bread to rise when baking.

4 Place the dough onto a baking sheet lined with parchment paper, and cook in the middle of the oven for 30 minutes to create a good crust. Reduce the oven temperature to 400°F (200°C), and bake for another 20 minutes until well risen, golden brown, and a skewer inserted into the middle emerges clean. Transfer the bread to a wire rack and allow it to cool for at least 20 minutes before serving.

STORE This bread will keep, well wrapped in paper, for 3 days.

Parsnip and Parmesan Bread

A perfect combination of flavors to serve with a bowl of warm soup on a cold winter's day.

| MAKES 1 LOAF | 20 MINS | 50 MINS | UP TO 8 WEEKS |

Ingredients

1½ cups all-purpose flour, plus extra for dusting
¾ cup whole wheat flour
1 tsp baking soda
½ tsp fine salt
freshly ground black pepper
2oz (50g) Parmesan cheese, finely grated
6oz (150g) parsnip
1¼ cups buttermilk

Method

1 Preheat the oven to 425°F (220°C). Mix together the all-purpose flour, whole wheat flour, baking soda, salt, pepper, and Parmesan. Grate the parsnip, then chop it coarsely to reduce the size of the shreds. Add it to the bowl, mixing well so no clumps form.

2 Make a well in the center of the dry ingredients and stir in the buttermilk to form a loose, ragged dough. Use your hands to bring the mixture together into a ball, then turn it out onto a lightly floured work surface and knead it for 2 minutes until it forms a smooth dough. You may need to add a little extra flour at this stage, depending on the water content of your vegetables.

3 Shape the dough into a round about 6in (15cm) in diameter, and slash the top with a cross to allow the bread to rise when baking. Place the dough onto a baking sheet lined with parchment paper and cook in the middle of the oven for 30 minutes to create a good crust. Reduce the oven temperature to 400°F (200°C), and bake for another 20 minutes until well risen, golden brown, and a skewer inserted into the middle emerges clean. Transfer the bread to a wire rack and let cool for at least 20 minutes before serving.

STORE This bread will keep, well wrapped in paper, for 3 days.

Cornbread

Cornbread is a traditional American loaf that makes a quick and easy accompaniment to soups and stews.

SERVES 8 | 15–20 MINS | 20–25 MINS

Special equipment
9in (23cm) flameproof cast-iron frying pan
loose-bottomed round cake pan

Ingredients
2 fresh corn cobs, about 7oz (200g) weight of kernels
4 tbsp unsalted butter or bacon drippings, melted and cooled, plus extra for greasing
1¼ cups fine yellow cornmeal or polenta
¾ cup bread flour
¼ cup sugar
1 tbsp baking powder
1 tsp salt
2 large eggs
1¼ cups milk

1 Preheat the oven to 425°F (220°C). Oil the pan with butter or bacon drippings. Place in oven.

2 Cut away the kernels from the cobs and scrape out the pulp with the back of the knife.

3 Sift the cornmeal, flour, sugar, baking powder, and salt into a bowl. Add the corn.

4 In a bowl, whisk together the eggs, melted butter or bacon drippings, and milk.

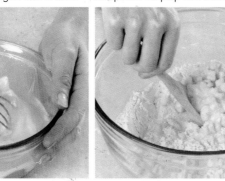

5 Pour three-quarters of the milk mixture into the flour mixture and stir.

6 Draw in the dry ingredients, adding the remaining milk mixture. Stir just until smooth.

7 Carefully take the hot pan out of the oven and pour in the batter; it should sizzle.

8 Quickly brush the top with butter or bacon drippings. Bake for 20–25 minutes.

9 The bread should shrink from the sides of the pan and a skewer should come out clean.

QUICK BREADS AND BATTERS

126

10 Let the cornbread cool slightly on a wire rack. Serve warm, with soup, chili con carne, or fried chicken. The cornbread does not keep well but leftovers can be used as a stuffing for roast poultry.

Cornbread variations

Corn Muffins with Roasted Red Pepper

In the spirit of the American West, sweet red pepper is roasted, diced, and stirred into a corn batter. Baking the cornbread in muffin pans makes it easily portable for a picnic, packed lunch, or buffet.

MAKES 12 · 20 MINS · 15–20 MINS

Special equipment
12-hole muffin pan

Ingredients
1 large red bell pepper
1¼ cups fine yellow cornmeal
¾ cup bread flour
1 tbsp sugar
1 tbsp baking powder
1 tsp salt
2 large eggs
4 tbsp unsalted butter or bacon drippings, plus extra for greasing
1¼ cups milk

Method

1 Heat the broiler. Set the pepper underneath and broil, turning as needed, until the skin blackens and blisters. Put the pepper in a plastic bag, close it, and let cool. Peel off the skin and out the core. Cut the pepper in half and scrape out the seeds and ribs. Dice the flesh finely.

2 Preheat the oven to 425°F (220°C). Generously grease the muffin pan and place it in the oven to heat up. Sift the cornmeal, flour, sugar, baking powder, and salt into a large bowl, and make a well in the center. In a bowl, whisk together the eggs, melted butter or bacon drippings, and milk. Pour three-quarters of the milk mixture into the well in the flour, and stir. Gradually draw in the dry ingredients, adding the remaining milk mixture, and stirring just until smooth. Stir in the diced pepper.

3 Carefully remove the hot pan from the oven and spoon the batter into the muffin holes. Bake in the oven for 15–20 minutes, until they start to shrink from the sides of the holes and a metal skewer inserted in the center of a muffin comes out clean. Unmold the muffins and let cool slightly.

PREPARE AHEAD Best served warm from the oven, these can be made 1 day ahead and kept tightly wrapped in paper. If possible, warm gently in the oven before serving.

Southern-style Cornbread

This quick cornbread is traditionally served as an accompaniment for a barbecue, soup, or stew. Some authentic Southern recipes omit the honey. ▶

SERVES 8 · 10–15 MINS · 25–35 MINS

Special equipment
8in (20cm) springform round cake pan or similar-sized flameproof cast-iron frying pan

Ingredients
1⅔ cups fine cornmeal or polenta, ideally white cornmeal if you can get it
2 tsp baking powder
½ tsp fine salt
2 large eggs
1 cup buttermilk
4 tbsp unsalted butter or bacon drippings, melted and cooled, plus extra for greasing
1 tbsp honey (optional)

Method

1 Preheat the oven to 425°F (220°C). Grease the cake pan or frying pan and place it in the oven to heat up. In a large bowl, mix together the cornmeal, baking powder, and salt. Whisk together the eggs and buttermilk.

2 Make a well in the center of the cornmeal mixture and gradually pour in the buttermilk mixture, slowly stirring until incorporated. Stir in the melted butter or bacon drippings, and honey, if using, and mix until smooth.

3 Carefully remove the hot pan from the oven and pour in the mixture. The pan should be hot enough to make the batter sizzle as it goes in; this is what gives the cornbread its distinctive crust.

4 Bake in the middle of the oven for 20–25 minutes until slightly risen and browning at the edges. Leave to cool for 5 minutes.

PREPARE AHEAD Best served warm from the oven, the bread can be made 1 day ahead and kept tightly wrapped in paper.

ALSO TRY...

Chile and Cilantro Cornbread
Add 1 red chile, seeded and finely chopped, and 4 tablespoons finely chopped cilantro at the same time as the honey.

BAKER'S TIP
Southern cornbread gains a lot of its flavor from the use of melted bacon drippings in the batter, and a jar of collected leftover bacon grease is a common sight in kitchens across the Southern United States for this very reason—so start your own collection!

Buttermilk Biscuits

A favorite dish in the South, where biscuits are eaten for breakfast spread with something sweet or to accompany sausage gravy.

MAKES 12   **10 MINS**   **15 MINS**   **UP TO 4 WEEKS**

Special equipment
2½in (6cm) pastry cutter

Ingredients
1⅓ cups self-rising flour
1 tsp baking powder
½ tsp fine salt
7 tbsp unsalted butter, softened
1½ cups buttermilk, plus extra for brushing
1 tbsp honey

Method

1 Preheat the oven to 400°F (200°C). Sift the flour and baking powder into a bowl and add the salt. With your fingertips, rub the butter into the dry ingredients until the mixture resembles fine crumbs.

2 Make a well in the center and pour in the buttermilk and honey. Work the mixture together to form a rough dough, then turn it out onto a lightly floured work surface and bring it together into a smooth ball. Do not over handle it or the biscuits may harden (see Baker's Tip).

3 Roll out the dough to a thickness of ¾in (2cm) and cut 2½in (6cm) biscuits out of it with the pastry cutter. Gather up the remaining dough, re-roll it, and cut out biscuits until all the dough is used up.

4 Place the biscuits on a non-stick baking sheet and brush the tops with buttermilk, to give them a golden finish. Bake in the top third of the oven for 15 minutes until golden brown and well risen. Remove from the oven and cool for 5 minutes on a wire rack before serving, still warm.

STORE The biscuits can be kept in an airtight container for 1 day and warmed up again in the oven before serving.

BAKER'S TIP
Buttermilk biscuits have a tendency to harden and taste tough if overhandled. To avoid this, bring the mix together gently and stop as soon as it forms a dough. When rolling gently, try to cut out as many biscuits from the first rolling as possible, as biscuits from subsequent rollings will be tougher.

Blueberry Pancakes

Dropping the blueberries on top of the half-cooked pancakes stops the juice from leaking into the pan and burning.

MAKES 30 | 10 MINS | 15–20 MINS

Ingredients

2 tbsp unsalted butter, plus extra
  for cooking and to serve
2 large eggs
1½ cups all-purpose flour
1½ tsp baking powder

2 tbsp sugar
¼ teaspoon salt
1 cup milk
1 tsp pure vanilla extract
6oz (150g) blueberries
maple syrup, to serve

QUICK BREADS AND BATTERS

1 Melt the butter in a small saucepan and set aside to cool.

2 Crack the eggs into a small bowl and lightly beat with a fork until combined.

3 Sift the flour and baking powder into a bowl, lifting the sieve high above to aerate the flour.

4 Stir in the sugar and salt until evenly and thoroughly mixed with the flour.

5 In a large measuring cup, beat together the milk, eggs, and vanilla, until well blended.

6 With a spoon, form a well in the center of the dry ingredients.

7 Pour a little of the egg mixture into the well and start to whisk it in.

8 Wait until each addition of egg mixture has been incorporated before whisking in more.

9 Finally, whisk in the melted butter until the mixture is entirely smooth.

10 Melt a knob of butter in a large, non-stick frying pan over medium heat.

11 Pour 1 tablespoon of the batter into the pan, to form a round pancake.

12 Continue to add tablespoons of batter, leaving space between for them to spread.

13 As they begin to cook, sprinkle a few blueberries over the uncooked surface.

14 They are ready to turn when small bubbles appear and pop, leaving small holes.

15 Turn the pancakes over carefully with a metal spatula.

16 Continue to cook for a minute or two until golden brown on both sides and cooked.

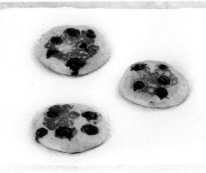

17 Remove the pancakes from the pan and drain briefly on paper towels.

18 Place the pancakes on a plate and transfer to a warm oven.

19 Wipe out the frying pan with paper towels, and add another tablespoon of butter.

20 Repeat for all the batter and wipe between batches. The pan should not get too hot.

21 Remove the pancakes from the oven. Serve warm in stacks, with butter and maple syrup.

Pancake variations

Cinnamon Pancakes

Transform any leftover pancakes with this quick topping.

MAKES 8   **10 MINS**   **5 MINS**

Ingredients
1 tsp ground cinnamon
¼ cup sugar
8 leftover pancakes, see Blueberry Pancakes, pages 132–133
2 tbsp unsalted butter, melted

Method
1 Preheat the broiler. Mix the cinnamon and sugar together and pour onto a plate. Brush each pancake on both sides with melted butter and press each side into the sugar and cinnamon mix, shaking off the excess sugar.

2 Place the pancakes on a baking sheet and cook under the hot broiler until the sugar is bubbling and melted. Leave the sugar to set for 1 minute before turning them over and broiling on the other side. Serve immediately with Greek yogurt, or just plain as an afternoon snack.

Drop Scones

So-called because the batter is dropped onto a frying pan.

MAKES 12   **10 MINS**   **15 MINS**   **UP TO 4 WEEKS**

Ingredients
1⅓ cup all-purpose flour
4 tsp baking powder
1 large egg
2 tsp corn syrup
¾ cup milk, plus extra if needed
vegetable oil

Method
1 Place a flat griddle pan or large frying pan over medium heat. Fold a kitchen towel in half and lay it on a baking sheet.

2 Sift the flour and baking powder into a bowl; make a well in the center, and add the egg, corn syrup, and milk. Whisk well to make a smooth batter the consistency of thick cream. If the mixture is too thick, beat in a little more milk.

3 Test that the griddle pan is hot enough by sprinkling a little flour onto the hot surface. If it burns, the pan is too hot. When the temperature is right, dust off the flour and rub a paper towel dipped in cooking oil lightly over the surface.

4 Lift out 1 tablespoon of batter. Drop the batter from the tip of the spoon onto the hot pan to make a nice round shape. Repeat, leaving enough room between the rounds for the pancakes to rise and spread.

5 Bubbles will appear on the surface of the pancakes. When they begin to burst, ease a spatula underneath the pancakes and flip to cook the other side. Place cooked pancakes inside the folded towel to keep them soft while you cook the rest of the batch.

6 Oil the hot pan after each batch and watch the heat. If the pancakes are pale and take a long time to cook, increase the heat. If they brown too quickly on the outside and are still raw in the middle, reduce the heat. These are best eaten freshly baked and warm.

Banana, Yogurt, and Honey Pancake Stack

Try stacking pancakes for a luxurious breakfast treat. ▶

SERVES 6   **10 MINS**   **15–20 MINS**

Ingredients
1 cup all-purpose flour
1 tsp baking powder
¼ cup sugar
1 cup whole milk
2 large eggs, beaten
½ tsp pure vanilla extract
2 tbsp unsalted butter, melted and cooled, plus extra for cooking
1 large banana
7oz (200g) Greek yogurt
honey, to serve

Method
1 Sift the flour and baking powder into a large bowl. Add the sugar. In a large measuring cup or pitcher whisk together the milk, eggs, and vanilla. Make a well in the center of the flour mixture and whisk in the milk mixture, a little at a time. Whisk in the butter until the mixture is entirely smooth.

2 Melt a tablespoon of butter in a large, non-stick frying pan. Pour tablespoons of the pancake batter into the pan, leaving space between them for the pancakes to spread. The pancakes should spread to be approximately 3¼-4in (8-10cm) in diameter. Cook the pancakes over medium heat. Turn the pancakes when small bubbles begin to appear on the surface and pop. Cook for another minute or 2 until golden brown on both sides and cooked through.

3 Slice the banana diagonally to produce 2in (5cm) long strips. Place 1 warm pancake on a plate. Top with a spoonful of Greek yogurt and some slices of banana. Top with another pancake, more yogurt, and honey. Finish the stack with a third pancake, topped with a spoonful of yogurt and drizzled generously with honey.

Crumpets

Eaten for breakfast or as an afternoon snack, toasted crumpets are great with both sweet and savory toppings.

**MAKES
8**

**10
MINS**

**20–26
MINS**

**UP TO 4
WEEKS**

Special equipment
4 crumpet rings, or 4in (10cm)
metal pastry cutters

Ingredients
1 cup all-purpose flour
¾ cup bread flour
½ tsp dried yeast
⅔ cup tepid milk
½ tsp salt
½ tsp baking soda
vegetable oil, for greasing

Method

1 Mix together the flours and yeast. Stir in the milk and ⅔ cup tepid water, and leave for 2 hours, or until the bubbles have risen and then started to fall again. Mix the salt and baking soda into 2 tablespoons lukewarm water and whisk in. Set aside for 5 minutes.

2 Oil the crumpet rings or pastry cutters. Lightly omeil a large, heavy frying pan and place the rings in the pan.

3 Pour the batter into a large measuring cup or pitcher. Heat the pan over medium heat and pour batter into each ring to a depth of ½-¾in (1-2cm). Cook the crumpets for 8–10 minutes, or until the batter has set all the way through and the top is covered in holes. If no bubbles appear, the mixture is too dry, so stir a little water into the remaining batter.

4 Lift the rings off the crumpets, turn them over, and cook for another 2–3 minutes, or until just golden. Repeat with the remaining batter. Serve the freshly cooked crumpets warm and buttered, or toast to reheat if serving them later.

BAKER'S TIP

The holes on top of crumpets are their unique selling point, making them the perfect repository for butter, jam, or marmalade. The leavening creates bubbles as they cook, which burst to produce these holes. Homemade crumpets tend to have fewer holes, but are no less tasty or absorbent for it.

Crêpes Suzette

In this most classic of French desserts, crêpes are flambéd just before serving. A sure way to create culinary drama.

SERVES
6

40–50
MINS

45–60
MINS

Standing time
30 mins

Ingredients

For the crêpes
1 cup all-purpose flour, sifted
1 tbsp sugar
½ tsp salt
4 large eggs, at room temperature
1½ cups milk, plus extra if needed
6 tbsp unsalted butter, melted and
  cooled, plus extra if needed

For the orange butter
12 tbsp unsalted butter,
  at room temperature
⅓ cup confectioner's sugar
3 large oranges, 2 finely grated and
  1 peeled with a vegetable peeler
  then cut into julienne strips
1 tbsp Grand Marnier

For flaming
⅓ cup brandy
⅓ cup Grand Marnier

1 Mix the flour, sugar, and salt. Make a well in the center, and add the eggs and half the milk.

2 Whisk, drawing in the flour, to make a batter. Whisk in half the butter, until smooth.

3 Add milk to give the batter the consistency of half-and-half. Cover and leave for 30 minutes.

4 For the orange butter, cream the butter and confectioner's sugar with a hand mixer.

5 With a sharp knife, cut the pith and skin from all 3 oranges.

6 Slide the knife down both sides of each segment to cut it free. Set aside.

7 Add the zest and 2 tablespoons juice to the butter with the Grand Marnier. Whisk well.

8 Add the julienned orange to a saucepan of boiling water; simmer for 2 minutes. Drain.

9 Add a little melted butter to a small frying pan and heat over medium-high heat.

10 Ladle 2–3 tablespoons of the batter into the pan, tilting the pan so the base is covered.

11 Fry for 1 minute. Gently loosen with a palette knife. Turn and cook for 30–60 seconds.

12 Repeat, adding butter only when the crêpes start to stick, making 12 crêpes.

13 Spread the orange butter over 1 side of each crêpe. Heat the pan over medium heat.

14 Add 1 crêpe at a time, butter-side down. Cook for 1 minute and fold into quarters.

15 Arrange the crêpes in the hot frying pan. Heat the alcohol, then pour over the crêpes.

16 Stand back. Hold a lighted match to the side of the pan. Baste until the flames die down.

17 Divide the crêpes among warmed plates and spoon the sauce from the pan over them.

18 Decorate with orange segments and strips, and serve. **PREPARE AHEAD** The plain crêpes can be made 3 days ahead, layered with parchment, and stored, wrapped, in the refrigerator.

Crêpe variations

Buckwheat Galettes

These savory pancakes are popular in the Brittany region of France, where the local cuisine is defined by rich, rustic flavors.

SERVES 4	25 MINS	25–30 MINS	12 WEEKS, UNFILLED

Resting time
2 hrs

Ingredients

For the galettes
½ cup buckwheat flour
½ cup all-purpose flour
2 large eggs, beaten
1 cup milk
sunflower or vegetable oil, for greasing

For the filling
2 tbsp sunflower or vegetable oil
2 red onions, peeled and thinly sliced
7oz (200g) smoked ham, chopped
1 tsp thyme leaves
4oz (115g) Brie cheese, cut into small pieces
½ cup crème fraîche

Method

1 Sift the flours into a large mixing bowl, make a well in the center, and add the eggs. Gradually beat the eggs into the flour using a wooden spoon, then add the milk and ½ cup water to make a smooth batter. Cover and let stand for 2 hours.

2 Heat the oil for the filling in a small frying pan, add the onions, and cook gently until softened. Add the ham and thyme, then remove from the heat and set aside.

3 Preheat the oven to 300°F (150°C). Heat the crêpe pan and grease lightly. Spoon in 2 tablespoons of batter and swirl so it coats the base of the pan. Cook for 1 minute, or until lightly browned underneath, then flip over and cook for another 1 minute, or until browned on the other side. Make 7 more crêpes, re-greasing the pan as necessary.

4 Stir the Brie and crème fraîche into the filling and divide between the pancakes. Roll or fold up the filled pancakes and place on a baking sheet. Heat through in the oven for 10 minutes before serving.

PREPARE AHEAD Make the batter a few hours in advance and leave to stand until ready to cook. If it thickens too much, stir in a little water before using.

Spinach, Pancetta, and Ricotta Pancake Bake

Try making with store-bought pancakes for a speedy supper.

SERVES 4	30 MINS	35 MINS	12 WEEKS, UNBAKED

Special equipment
9 x 13in (23 x 33cm) shallow ovenproof dish

Ingredients

For the batter
1¼ cups all-purpose flour
½ tsp fine salt
1 cup whole milk, plus extra if needed
4 large eggs
4 tbsp unsalted butter, melted and cooled, plus extra for cooking and greasing

For the filling
½ cup pine nuts
2 tsp extra virgin olive oil, plus extra for greasing
1 red onion, finely chopped
4oz (100g) diced pancetta
2 garlic cloves, crushed
10oz (300g) baby spinach, washed and dried
9oz (250g) ricotta
3–4 tbsp heavy cream
sea salt
freshly ground black pepper

For the cheese sauce
1½ cups heavy cream
2oz (60g) Parmesan cheese, finely grated

Method

1 Mix the flour and salt in a large bowl. Separately whisk together the milk and eggs. Make a well in the center of the flour mixture and whisk in the milk mixture, a little at a time, until it is all incorporated. Add the butter and whisk until entirely smooth. The mixture should be the consistency of pouring cream. Add extra milk if needed. Transfer to a large measuring cup or pitcher, cover with plastic wrap, and leave to rest for 30 minutes.

2 To make the filling, dry fry the pine nuts in a large sauté pan for 2 minutes over medium heat, turning often until they turn golden brown in places. Set aside.

3 Add the olive oil to the pan and sauté the onion for 3 minutes until softened, but not brown. Add the pancetta and cook it over medium heat for another 5 minutes, until golden brown and crispy. Add the garlic and cook for another minute. Add the baby spinach in handfuls; it will wilt down very quickly. Cook the spinach only until it begins to wilt, then take the pan from the heat.

4 Place the spinach mixture into a sieve, and press down with the back of a spoon to remove excess water. Transfer to a bowl, add the pine nuts, and mix with the ricotta and the cream. Season well and set aside.

5 Melt a tablespoon of butter in a large, non-stick frying pan, and when it begins to sizzle wipe away any excess with a piece of paper towel. Pour a couple of tablespoonfuls of the pancake mixture into the frying pan, and then tip the pan to cover with a thin layer of the batter. Cook for a couple of minutes on each side, turning them when the first side is golden brown. Set the cooked pancakes aside and continue until all the batter has been used up, adding a tablespoon more butter when necessary. This should give you approximately 10 pancakes.

6 Preheat the oven to 400°F (200°C). Lay a pancake out flat. Put 2 tablespoons of filling into the middle of the pancake. Use the back of the spoon to spread it out into a thick line, then roll the pancake up around it. Grease the dish and lay the pancakes side by side in the dish.

7 For the sauce, heat the heavy cream until nearly boiling. Add nearly all the Parmesan. Whisk until the cheese melts, then bring to a boil and simmer for 2 minutes until it thickens slightly. Season to taste and pour over the pancakes. Top with the reserved cheese.

8 Bake at the top of the oven for 20 minutes until golden and bubbling in places. Remove and serve immediately with a green salad.

PREPARE AHEAD This can be made up to the end of step 6, covered, and refrigerated for up to 2 days, before finishing with the sauce and baking as described.

Swedish Pancake Stack Cake

Make sure you use only the thinnest of crêpes for this sumptuous dessert. A perfect summer birthday cake and a children's favorite.

SERVES 6–8 | 10 MINS | 15 MINS

Ingredients
6 pancakes, made using ½ quantity crêpe batter, see pages 140–141, steps 1–3 and 10–12
¾ cup heavy cream
1 cup crème fraîche
3 tbsp sugar
¼ tsp pure vanilla extract
9oz (250g) raspberries
confectioner's sugar, to serve

Method
1 Whip the cream into stiff peaks. Combine the whipped cream, crème fraîche, sugar, and vanilla, and whisk until well mixed. Set aside ¼ cup to decorate the top of the cake.

2 Reserve a good handful of the raspberries. Lightly crush the remaining fruit with a fork and add them to the remaining cream mixture, folding them through roughly to create a rippled effect.

3 Place the first pancake on a serving platter, and spread one-fifth of the raspberry and cream mixture over the surface. Continue to layer until all the pancakes and cream are used up.

4 Top with the reserved cream mixture and the remaining raspberries. Dust with confectioner's sugar, and serve.

BAKER'S TIP
This stack cake is extremely versatile. You can try using chopped strawberries or blueberries, which will make an equally delicious cake. In Sweden, lingonberry jam (similar to sweet cranberry sauce) is often used as a substitute for the fresh fruit. You can find the jam in Scandinavian delicatessens.

Staffordshire Oatcakes

These oat pancakes can have sweet or savory fillings, can be folded in half, rolled up, or cooked on top of each other, then sliced in quarters.

MAKES 10 | 10 MINS | 15 MINS

Resting time
1–2 hrs

Ingredients
1 cup oat bran
1 cup whole wheat flour
1 cup all-purpose flour
½ tsp fine salt
2 tsp dried yeast
1¼ cups milk
unsalted butter, for frying

For the filling
9oz (250g) cheese, such as Cheddar
  or red Leicester, grated
20 slices bacon

Method

1 Sift together the oat bran, whole wheat flour, all-purpose flour, and salt. Add the dried yeast to 1¾ cups warm water and whisk well until it is completely dissolved. Add the milk. Make a well in the center of the dry ingredients and stir in the milk and water mixture.

2 Whisk the mixture together until the batter is completely smooth. Cover and set aside for 1–2 hours, until small bubbles start to appear on the surface of the batter.

3 Melt a tablespoon of butter in a large, non-stick frying pan and, when it begins to sizzle, wipe any excess away quickly with a piece of paper towel.

4 Pour a ladleful of the oatcake mixture into the center of the frying pan, and then tip the pan to allow the batter to spread all around. The idea is to cover the surface of the pan very quickly with a thin layer of the batter.

5 Cook the oatcakes for a couple of minutes on each side, turning them when the edges are cooked through and the first side is golden brown. Set the cooked oatcakes aside in a warm place and continue until all the batter has been used up.

6 Meanwhile, preheat the broiler and broil the bacon. Sprinkle a handful of grated cheese all over the surface of an oatcake.

7 Place it under the broiler for a couple of minutes until the cheese has completely melted. Place 2 slices of bacon on top of the melted cheese to 1 side of the oatcake, and roll it up before serving.

BAKER'S TIP
These traditional oatcakes are really savory pancakes, though a little more wholesome, and make a fantastic breakfast treat every once in a while. For an even quicker breakfast, the batter can be made the night before and stored, covered, in the refrigerator overnight.

QUICK BREADS AND BATTERS

Blinis

These buckwheat-based pancakes originated in Russia. Try serving them as canapés, or larger topped with smoked fish and crème fraîche for lunch.

MAKES 48 BLINIS | **20 MINS** | **15 MINS** | **UP TO 8 WEEKS**

Resting time
2 hrs

Ingredients

½ tsp dried yeast
¾ cup warm milk
½ cup sour cream
1 cup buckwheat flour
1 cup bread flour
½ tsp fine salt
2 large eggs, separated
4 tbsp butter, melted and cooled, plus extra for cooking

Method

1 Mix the yeast with the warm milk and whisk until the yeast dissolves. Whisk in the sour cream and set aside.

2 In a large bowl, mix together the 2 types of flour and the salt. Make a well in the center of the flour mixture and gradually whisk in the milk and sour cream. Add the egg yolks and continue to whisk. Finally add the butter and whisk until smooth.

3 Cover the bowl with plastic wrap and set aside in a warm place for at least 1 hour, until bubbles appear all over the surface.

4 In a clean bowl whisk the egg whites to soft peaks. Add the egg whites to the batter and gently fold them in using a metal spoon or spatula, until they are well combined and there are no lumps of egg white. Transfer the batter to a large measuring cup or pitcher.

5 Heat a tablespoon of butter in a large, non-stick frying pan. Pour 1 tablespoon of the batter at a time into the pan to form small blinis approximately 2½in (6cm) in diameter. Cook the blinis for a minute or 2 over medium heat until bubbles start to appear on the surface. When the bubbles begin to pop, turn and cook for a minute on the second side. Remove the blinis to a warm plate, cover with a clean kitchen towel, and continue to cook until all the batter is used up.

6 Serve the blinis still warm, with sour cream and smoked salmon for a delicious canapé. They can also be wrapped in foil and gently reheated in a warm oven for 10 minutes before serving.

PREPARE AHEAD The blinis will keep in an airtight container in the refrigerator for up to 3 days. Reheat them (from fresh or frozen) as in step 6.

BAKER'S TIP

Blinis are simple to make, but can be difficult to get perfectly circular, and small enough to serve as a canapé. Remember to pour the batter directly into the center of the blini, and use a spoon to catch any drips from the pitcher as you finish pouring.

Cherry Clafoutis

This French favorite can be enjoyed warm or at room temperature.

SERVES 6 | 12 MINS | 35–45 MINS

Resting time
30 mins

Special equipment
10in (25cm) tart pan or shallow
ovenproof dish

Ingredients
1lb 10oz (750g) cherries
3 tbsp Kirsch
⅓ cup sugar
unsalted butter, for greasing

4 large eggs, at room temperature
1 vanilla bean (optional)
¾ cup all-purpose flour
1¼ cups milk
pinch of salt

QUICK BREADS AND BATTERS

1 Toss the cherries with the Kirsch and 2 tablespoons sugar. Leave for 30 minutes.

2 Preheat the oven to 400°F (200°C). Butter the tart pan and set aside.

3 Strain the liquid from the cherries into a large bowl. Set the cherries aside.

4 Beat the eggs into the Kirsch mixture, until very well amalgamated.

5 With a sharp knife, split the vanilla bean (if using) vertically down the middle.

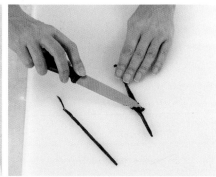

6 Run the tip of the knife down the middle of each half to scrape out all the seeds.

7 Add the seeds to the egg and Kirsch mixture and mix well to distribute.

8 Add the remaining sugar and beat well to combine.

9 Sift the flour into a large bowl, lifting the sieve high to aerate the flour as it floats down.

10 Beat the flour into the egg mixture, whisking after each addition, to make a smooth paste.

11 Pour in the milk, add the salt, and whisk until it makes a smooth batter.

12 Arrange the cherries in 1 layer in the tart dish. They should fill the dish.

13 Slowly pour the batter over the top of the cherries, trying not to displace the cherries.

14 Bake for 35–45 minutes, or until the top is browned and the center is firm to the touch.

15 Allow to cool on a wire rack. Dust with confectioner's sugar and remove from the pan.

16 Serve warm or at room temperature, with plenty of thick cream or crème fraîche for spooning over, or with vanilla ice cream.

Clafoutis variations

Toad in the Hole

This classic British version of clafoutis is perfect comfort food.

SERVES 4 | 20 MINS | 35–40 MINS

Standing time
30 mins

Special equipment
roasting pan or shallow ovenproof dish

Ingredients
1 cup all-purpose flour
pinch of salt
2 large eggs
1¼ cups milk
2 tbsp vegetable oil
8 Toulouse or Italian sausages

Method

1 To make the batter, put the flour into a bowl with the salt, make a well in the center, and add the eggs with a little of the milk. Whisk together, gradually incorporating the flour. Add the remaining milk and whisk to make a smooth batter. Leave to rest for at least 30 minutes.

2 Preheat the oven to 425°F (220°C). Heat the oil in a roasting pan or shallow ovenproof dish. Add the sausages and toss them in the hot oil. Bake for 5–10 minutes, or until the sausages are just colored and the fat is very hot.

3 Reduce the oven temperature to 400°F (200°C). Carefully pour the batter around the sausages and return to the oven for another 30 minutes, until the batter is risen, golden, and crisp. Serve immediately, with onion gravy, green vegetables, and mustard.

PREPARE AHEAD The batter can be made 24 hours in advance. Keep chilled and whisk briefly just before using.

Apricot Clafoutis

This French favorite can be enjoyed warm or at room temperature. Canned apricots taste just fine when fresh are out of season.

SERVES 4 | 10 MINS | 35 MINS

Special equipment
shallow ovenproof dish

Ingredients
unsalted butter, for greasing
1 can of apricot halves, drained, or 9oz (250g) fresh ripe apricots, halved and pitted
1 large egg, plus 1 large egg yolk
2 tbsp all-purpose flour
¼ cup sugar
⅔ cup heavy cream
¼ tsp pure vanilla extract

Method

1 Preheat the oven to 400°F (200°C). Lightly grease the dish; it should be big enough to fit the apricots in a single layer. Place the apricots cut side down in a single layer in the dish; there should be spaces between them.

2 In a bowl whisk together the egg and egg yolk and the flour. Whisk in the sugar. Finally add the cream and vanilla extract and whisk thoroughly to a smooth custard.

3 Pour the custard around the apricots. The tops of the apricots should be just visible here and there above the custard.

4 Bake in the top of the preheated oven for 35 minutes until puffed up and golden brown in places. Remove from the oven and allow to cool for at least 15 minutes. This clafoutis is best served warm with thick cream or crème fraîche.

PREPARE AHEAD This dessert is best freshly baked and served warm, but can also be cooked up to 6 hours ahead and served at room temperature.

Plum and Marzipan Clafoutis

This stunning version is equally good made with plums or cherries, but instead of putting the marzipan in the fruit cavities, dot little pieces between each fruit.

SERVES 6   **30 MINS**   **50 MINS**

Special equipment
shallow ovenproof dish

Ingredients

For the marzipan
1 cup ground almonds
½ cup sugar
½ cup confectioner's sugar, plus extra for dusting
a few drops of almond extract
½ tsp lemon juice
1 large egg white, lightly beaten

For the clafoutis
1½lb (675g) plums, halved and pitted
5 tbsp butter
4 large eggs and 1 egg yolk
½ cup sugar
⅓ cup all-purpose flour, sifted
2 cups milk
⅔ cup half-and-half

Method

1 Preheat the oven to 375°F (190°C). Mix the marzipan ingredients together with enough of the egg white to form a stiff paste. Push a tiny piece of the paste into the cavity in each of the plum halves.

2 Grease a shallow, ovenproof dish, large enough to hold the plums in a single layer, with 1 tablespoon of the butter. Arrange the plums cut-side down in the dish, with the marzipan underneath. Melt the remaining butter and leave to cool.

3 Add any leftover egg white from the marzipan to the eggs and egg yolk. Add the sugar and whisk until thick and pale. Whisk in the melted butter, flour, milk, and half-and-half to form a batter. Pour over the plums and bake in the oven for about 50 minutes until golden and just set. Serve warm, dusted with confectioner's sugar.

PREPARE AHEAD The clafoutis is best freshly baked and served warm, but can be cooked up to 6 hours ahead and served at room temperature.

> **BAKER'S TIP**
> Clafoutis is basically a sweetened custard, baked around any type of seasonal fruit. As a pantry standby, try the classic version with canned apricots, but in season, you can use cherries, blackberries, plums, and black, white, or red currants.

Plum Clafoutis

This is a satisfying fall dessert to make, when the plums are at their peak. You can substitute plum or ordinary brandy for the Kirsch, if preferred. **PICTURED OVERLEAF**

SERVES 6–8   **20–25 MINS**   **30–35 MINS**

Special equipment
shallow ovenproof dish

Ingredients
unsalted butter, for greasing
½ cup sugar, plus extra for baking dish
1lb 6oz (625g) small plums, halved and pitted
2 tbsp all-purpose flour
salt
⅔ cup milk
⅓ cup heavy cream
4 large eggs, plus 2 large egg yolks
3 tbsp Kirsch
2 tbsp confectioner's sugar

Method

1 Preheat the oven to 350°F (180°C). Grease the baking dish with the butter. Sprinkle some sugar into the dish. Turn the dish around and shake it to coat the bottom and side evenly. Tap out any excess. Spread the plums, cut side up, evenly in the dish.

2 Sift the flour and a pinch of salt into a bowl and make a well in the center. Pour in the milk and cream and whisk, drawing in the flour, to make a smooth paste. Add the eggs, egg yolks, and sugar, and whisk to make a smooth batter.

3 Just before baking, ladle the batter over the plums, then spoon over the Kirsch. Bake the clafoutis in the oven for 30–35 minutes, until puffed up and beginning to brown. Just before serving, sift over the confectioner's sugar. Serve warm or at room temperature, with whipped cream.

PREPARE AHEAD The clafoutis is best freshly baked and served warm, but can be cooked up to 6 hours ahead and served at room temperature.

sweet breads

Brioche des Rois

This French bread is usually eaten for the Epiphany, January 6th. The *fève* represents the gifts of the Three Kings.

SERVES 10–12 | **25 MINS** | **25–30 MINS** | **UP TO 4 WEEKS**

Rising and proofing time
4–6 hrs

Special equipment
10in (25cm) ring mold (optional)
fève porcelain or metal trinket

Ingredients

For the brioche
1 (¼oz/10g) package dried yeast
2 tbsp sugar
5 large eggs, beaten

2¾ cups bread flour, extra for dusting
1½ tsp salt
oil, for greasing
12 tbsp unsalted butter,
  cubed and softened

For the topping
1 large egg, lightly beaten
⅓ cup (2oz) mixed candied fruit
  (orange and lemon zest, glacé
  cherries, and angelica), chopped
¼ cup coarse sugar crystals

1 Whisk yeast, 1 teaspoon sugar, 2 tablespoons warm water. Leave for 10 minutes. Add eggs.

2 In a large bowl, sift together the flour and salt, and add the remaining sugar.

3 Make a well in the flour and pour in the eggs and yeast mixture.

4 Bring the dough together with a fork, then your hands, to form a sticky dough.

5 Turn out the dough on to a floured work surface.

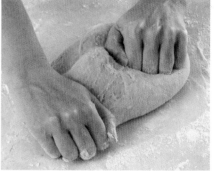

6 Knead the dough for 10 minutes until elastic but still sticky.

7 Put in an oiled bowl and cover with plastic wrap. Leave in a warm place for 2–3 hours.

8 Gently knock the dough back on a lightly floured work surface.

9 Scatter one-third of the cubed butter over the surface of the dough.

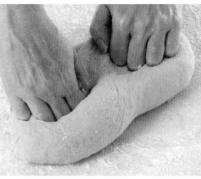

10 Fold the dough over the butter and knead gently for 5 minutes until all the butter is used.

11 Repeat until all the butter is absorbed. Keep kneading until no streaks of butter show.

12 Form into a round and work it into a ring. Bury the *fève*, if using (see Baker's Tip, page 159).

13 Transfer to an oiled baking sheet or fill an oiled ring mold, if using.

14 If you don't have a ring mold, use a ramekin to keep the shape of the hole.

15 Cover with plastic wrap and a kitchen towel and let rise for 2–3 hours until doubled in size.

16 Brush the brioche with beaten egg. Sprinkle with candied fruit and sugar crystals if using.

17 Preheat the oven to 400°F (200°C). Bake for 25–30 minutes until golden brown.

18 Leave in the pan for a few minutes, then turn out to cool on a wire rack, without dislodging the toppings. **STORE** This will keep in an airtight container for 3 days.

Brioche variations

Brioche Buns

These bite-sized little buns are known in French as brioche *à tête*, for obvious reasons.

MAKES 10 BUNS | **45–50 MINS** | **15–20 MINS** | **UP TO 8 WEEKS**

Rising and proofing time
1½–2 hrs

Special equipment
10 x 3in (7.5cm) brioche molds

Ingredients
butter, melted, for greasing
1 quantity brioche dough,
  see pages 156–157, steps 1–11
flour, for dusting
1 egg, beaten, for glazing
½ tsp salt, for glazing

Method

1 Grease the molds and set on a baking sheet. Divide the dough in half. Roll one piece into a cylinder 2in (5cm) in diameter. Cut the cylinder into 5 pieces. Repeat with the remaining dough. Flour the work surface, then roll the dough so it forms a smooth ball.

2 Pinch ¼ of each ball between your thumb and forefinger, almost dividing it from the remaining dough, to form the head. Lower each ball into a mold, twisting the head on to the base of the brioche. Cover and let rise for 30 minutes, until the molds are full.

3 Preheat the oven to 425°F (220°C). Brush with the egg glaze, and bake for 15–20 minutes, until puffed and brown. Unmold and transfer to a wire rack to cool.

STORE The buns will keep in an airtight container for 3 days.

Rum Babas

Rum soaked versions of brioche—perfect for a dinner party.

MAKES 4 BABAS | **20 MINS** | **20 MINS**

Rising time
30 mins

Special equipment
4 individual baba molds

Ingredients
¾ cup bread flour
¼ cup (2oz) raisins
1½ tsp dried yeast
2 tbsp sugar
pinch of salt
2 large eggs, at room temperature, lightly beaten
¼ cup milk, warmed
4 tbsp butter, melted, plus extra for greasing
vegetable oil, for greasing
½ cup sugar
3 tbsp rum
1¼ cups heavy whipping cream
2 tbsp confectioner's sugar
grated chocolate, to garnish

Method

1 Place the flour in a bowl and stir in the raisins, yeast, sugar, and salt. Beat together the egg and milk and add to the flour mixture. Stir in the melted butter. Beat well for 3–4 minutes then pour the mixture into well-greased baba molds to half fill them.

2 Place the molds on a baking sheet and cover with a sheet of oiled plastic wrap. Let rise in a warm place for 30 minutes. Preheat the oven to 400°F (200°C). Bake for 10–15 minutes, until golden and just firm to the touch. Let cool for a few minutes, then turn out on to a wire rack to cool completely.

3 Pour ½ cup of water into a saucepan and add the sugar. Stir constantly over low heat until the sugar dissolves. Increase the heat and boil rapidly for 2 minutes. Remove from the heat and leave to cool. Stir in the rum.

4 Dip the babas in the syrup. Whisk the cream and confectioner's sugar together until it forms soft peaks. Pipe a swirl of cream in the center of each baba. Sprinkle a little chocolate over the cream, and serve.

SWEET BREADS

Brioche Nanterre

Basic brioche dough can be baked into rings, buns, or loaves. This classic brioche loaf is best for slicing and fantastic toasted.

| MAKES 1 LOAF | 30 MINS | 25–30 MINS | UP TO 4 WEEKS |

Rising and proofing time
4–6 hrs

Special equipment
9 x 5½in (23 x 13cm) loaf pan

Ingredients
1 quantity brioche dough,
  see pages 156–157, steps 1–11
1 egg, beaten, for glazing

Method

1 Line the bottom and sides of the pan with parchment paper. Put a double layer on the base. Divide the dough into 8 pieces, and roll them up to form small balls. They should fit in pairs, side by side, in the base of the prepared pan.

2 Cover with plastic wrap and a kitchen towel, and let rise for another 2–3 hours until the dough has again doubled in size.

3 Preheat the oven to 400°F (200°C). Brush the top of the brioche loaf with a little beaten egg, and bake near the top of the oven for 30 minutes, or until the bottom of the loaf sounds hollow when tapped. Check the loaf after 20 minutes and cover the top with a piece of loose-fitting parchment paper if it is in danger of becoming too brown.

4 Leave to cool in the pan for a few minutes, then turn out to cool on a wire rack. This brioche is delicious toasted and buttered.

STORE The loaf will keep in an airtight container for 3 days.

BAKER'S TIP
Brioche originates from France, and was often made to celebrate Epiphany on January 6. Traditionally a *fève* is hidden in the dough, and the finder is guaranteed luck for the coming year. In the past a dried bean (*fève*) was used, but these days small decorative ceramic figures are more common.

Hefezopf

This traditional German bread is similar to brioche. Like all yeasted sweet breads, it is at its best the day of baking.

MAKES 1 LOAF | **20 MINS** | **25–35 MINS** | **UP TO 8 WEEKS**

Rising and proofing time
4–4½ hrs

Ingredients
1½ tsp dried yeast
1¼ cup warm milk
1 large egg
2½ cups all-purpose flour,
   plus extra for dusting
¼ cup sugar
¼ tsp fine salt

5 tbsp unsalted butter, melted
vegetable oil, for greasing
1 egg, beaten, for glazing

1 Dissolve the yeast in the warm milk. Let it cool, then add the egg and beat well.

2 Put the flour, sugar, and salt in a large bowl. Make a well and pour in the milk mixture.

3 Add the melted butter and gradually draw in the flour, stirring to form a soft dough.

4 Knead for 10 minutes on a floured surface, until smooth, soft, and pliable.

5 Put in an oiled bowl and cover with plastic wrap. Leave for 2–2½ hours until doubled.

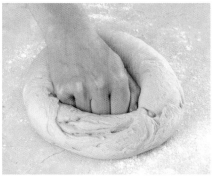

6 Put the dough on a floured work surface and gently knock it back. Divide into 3 equal pieces.

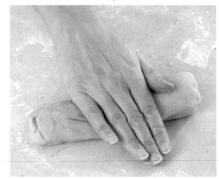

7 Take each piece of dough and roll it under your palm to make a fat log shape.

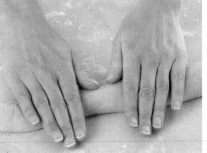

8 Using your palms, continue to roll it toward each end, until it is about 12in (30cm) long.

9 Pinch the tops of the 3 pieces together and tuck the ends underneath to start the braid.

SWEET BREADS

160

10 Loosely braid the dough, leaving room for it to rise. Pinch and tuck the ends underneath.

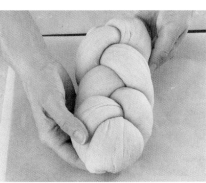

11 Put on a baking sheet lined with parchment. Cover with oiled plastic wrap and a towel.

12 Leave in a warm place for 2 hours; it will not double now, but will rise on baking.

13 Preheat the oven to 375°F (190°C). Brush liberally with beaten egg.

14 Bake for 25–30 minutes, until golden. Check if undercooked where the braids meet.

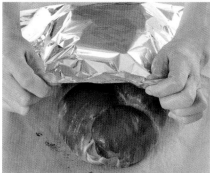

15 If undercooked, cover with foil and bake for 5 minutes. Cool for 15 minutes before serving.

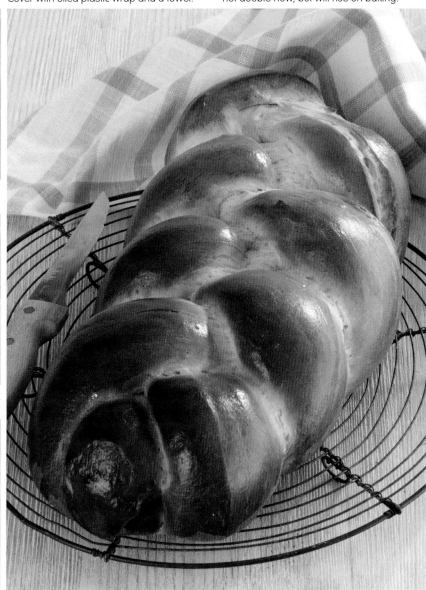

STORE Wrap in plastic wrap for 2 days. **ALSO TRY...** For variety, add 3oz (75g) golden raisins at step 2 and scatter 2 tablespoons sliced almonds after brushing with egg at step 13.

Hefezopf variations

Spiced Pecan and Raisin Hefezopf

The nuts and spices make this bread even tastier toasted.

| MAKES 1 LOAF | 30 MINS | 25–35 MINS | UP TO 8 WEEKS |

Rising and proofing time
4–4½ hrs

Ingredients
3 x "logs" hefezopf dough, approx. 12in (30cm) long, see page 160, steps 1–8
¼ cup raisins
¼ cup pecans, coarsely chopped
2 tbsp light brown sugar
1 tsp pumpkin pie spice

Method

1 Roll each "log" of dough out crosswise, so that you have three pieces each 12 x 3¼in (30 x 8cm). The measurements do not have to be precise, but the pieces of dough should be roughly the same shape.

2 Mix together the raisins, pecans, sugar, and pumpkin pie spice. Scatter a third of the mixture over each piece of dough, and press down with your palms firmly. Roll up each piece along its longest side, tucking the dough in firmly as you go. You should be left with three 12in (30cm) "ropes" of dough stuffed with the raisin and nut mix.

3 Pinch the tops of the 3 pieces of dough together and tuck the ends underneath. Now loosely braid the dough together, leaving room for it to rise, and pinch and tuck the ends underneath.

4 Transfer the loaf to a baking sheet lined with parchment paper, cover with lightly oiled plastic wrap and a kitchen towel, and leave in a warm place for another 2 hours. This dough will rise, but not double in size. Preheat the oven to 375°F (190°C).

5 Brush the loaf with egg, making sure to get into the ends of the braid. Bake in the preheated oven for 25–30 minutes, until well risen and golden brown. If the bread is undercooked where the braids meet, but

has browned well, cover loosely with foil and cook for another 5 minutes. Remove from the oven and leave to cool on a wire rack for at least 15 minutes before serving.

STORE This loaf is best eaten the day it is baked, but will store, wrapped in plastic wrap, for 2 days.

BAKER'S TIP

Hefezopf is a sweet yeasted bread, traditionally braided and baked at Easter all over Germany. It is quite similar to a brioche dough recipe, and can be baked plain or stuffed with a variety of dried fruits and nuts. Try experimenting with this recipe to include your favorites.

SWEET BREADS

Challah

This traditional Jewish bread is baked for holidays and the Sabbath.

MAKES 1 LOAF | **45–55 MINS** | **35–40 MINS** | **UP TO 8 WEEKS**

Proofing time
1¾–2¼ hrs

Ingredients
2½ tsp dried yeast
4 tbsp vegetable oil, plus extra for greasing
4 tbsp sugar
2 eggs, plus 1 yolk, for glazing
2 tsp salt
2¼ cups bread flour,
  plus extra for dusting
1 tsp poppy seeds, for sprinkling (optional)

Method

1 Put 1 cup of water into a pan and bring just to a boil. Pour 4 tablespoons into a bowl and let cool to lukewarm. Sprinkle over the yeast and let stand, stirring once, for 5 minutes, until dissolved. Add the oil and sugar to the remaining water in the pan and heat until melted. Let cool to lukewarm.

2 In a large bowl, beat the eggs just until mixed. Add the cooled sweetened water, salt, and dissolved yeast. Stir in half the flour and mix well. Add the remaining flour gradually, until the dough forms a ball. It should be soft and slightly sticky.

3 Turn onto a floured work surface. Knead for 5–7 minutes, until very smooth and elastic. Oil a large bowl. Put the dough in the bowl, and flip it. Cover with a damp kitchen towel and let rise in a warm place for 1–1½ hours, until doubled in bulk.

4 Lightly brush a baking sheet with oil. Turn the dough onto a lightly floured work surface and knock back. Cut the dough into 4 equal pieces. Flour the work surface. Roll each piece of dough with your hands to a 25in (63cm) strand.

5 Line the strands up next to each other. Starting from your left, lift the first strand to cross over the second. Lift the third strand to cross over the fourth. Now lift the fourth

strand and lay it between the first and second strands. Finish braiding the strands, pinching the ends together and tucking them under the braided loaf.

6 Transfer the loaf to the prepared baking sheet. Cover with a dry kitchen towel and let rise in a warm place for about 45 minutes, until doubled in bulk. Preheat the oven to 375°F (190°C). Make the glaze by beating the egg yolk with 1 tablespoon water until it looks frothy. Brush the loaf with the glaze, and sprinkle with poppy seeds, if you like.

7 Bake in the oven for 35–40 minutes, until golden and the bread sounds hollow when the bottom is tapped.

STORE Challah is best eaten the day it is made, but will store, wrapped in plastic wrap, for up to 2 days.

Pane al latte

This soft, slightly sweet Italian milk bread is perfect for small children—though adults will enjoy it for breakfast or lunch as well!

MAKES 1 LOAF | 30 MINS | 20 MINS

Rising and proofing time
2½–3 hrs

SWEET BREADS

Ingredients

4 cups all-purpose flour, plus extra for dusting
1 tsp salt
2 tbsp sugar
2 tsp dried yeast
¾ cup warm milk
2 large eggs, plus 1 egg, beaten, for glazing
4 tbsp unsalted butter, melted
vegetable oil, for greasing

Method

1 Put the flour, salt, and sugar into a bowl and mix well. Dissolve the yeast in the milk, whisking to help it dissolve. Once the liquid has cooled, add the eggs and beat well.

2 Gradually pour the milk mixture, then the butter, into the flour mixture, stirring it to form a soft dough. Knead the dough for 10 minutes on a floured work surface, until smooth, glossy, and elastic.

3 Put the dough in a lightly oiled bowl, cover loosely with plastic wrap, and leave to rise in a warm place for up to 2 hours, until doubled in size. Turn the dough out onto a lightly floured work surface and gently knock it back. Divide it into 5 roughly equal pieces. Ideally, 2 should be slightly bigger than the rest.

4 Knead each piece briefly, and roll it out to a long, fat log shape. The 3 smaller pieces should be about 8in (20cm) long, and the 2 larger ones about 10in (25cm) long. Take the 3 shorter pieces and position them side-by-side on a baking sheet

lined with parchment paper. Place the 2 longer ones on each side and draw the tops and bottoms together, flaring out the centers to form a "circle." Pinch the top of the loaf together to ensure that the dough does not come apart.

5 Cover it loosely with lightly oiled plastic wrap and a clean kitchen towel, and leave it in a warm place to rise, until almost doubled in size. This could take 30 minutes to 1 hour. Preheat the oven to 375°F (190°C).

6 Gently brush with a little beaten egg and bake for 20 minutes, until golden brown. Remove from the oven and leave to cool for at least 10 minutes before serving.

STORE Best eaten still warm from the oven, the bread can be wrapped in paper overnight and toasted the next day.

BAKER'S TIP

The use of eggs, milk, and sugar give this very soft Italian bread a sweet, gentle flavor and velvety texture. It toasts well, but is at its best served still warm with plenty of cold, unsalted butter and homemade strawberry jam. It is especially popular with children.

Panettone

A sweet bread eaten all over Italy at Christmas. Making one is not as hard as it seems, and the results are delicious.

SERVES 8 | 30 MINS | 40–45 MINS | UP TO 4 WEEKS

Rising and proofing time
4 hrs

Special equipment
High-sided panettone mold or 8in (20cm) springform cake pan

Ingredients

1½ tsp dried yeast
1 cup milk
¼ cup sugar
3¼ cups bread flour, plus extra for dusting
½ tsp salt
5 tbsp unsalted butter, melted
2 large eggs, plus 1 small egg at room temperature, beaten
1 tsp pure vanilla extract
1 cup (6oz) mixed dried fruit (cranberries, apricots, golden raisins, and mixed citrus peel), chopped
finely grated zest of 1 orange
vegetable oil, for greasing
confectioner's sugar, for dusting

1 Add the yeast to the warm milk in a jug. Mix the sugar, flour, and salt in a large bowl.

2 Once the yeasted milk is frothy (5 minutes), whisk in the butter, large eggs, and vanilla.

3 Mix the liquid and dry ingredients to form a soft dough; it will be stickier than bread dough.

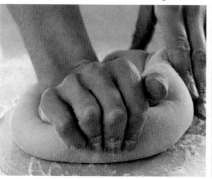

4 On a lightly floured surface, knead the dough for about 10 minutes until elastic.

5 Form the dough into a loose ball and stretch it out flat onto a floured work surface.

6 Scatter the dried fruit and orange zest on top and knead again until well combined.

7 Form the dough into a loose ball and put it in a lightly oiled bowl.

8 Cover the bowl with a damp, clean kitchen towel or place inside a large plastic bag.

9 Leave the dough to rise in a warm place for up to 2 hours, until doubled in size.

10 Line the pan with a double layer of parchment paper, or a layer of silicone paper.

11 If using a cake pan, form a collar with the paper, 2–4in (5–10cm) higher than the pan.

12 Knock the air out of the dough with your fist and turn out onto a lightly floured surface.

13 Knead the dough into a round ball just big enough to fit into the pan.

14 Put it into the pan, cover, and leave to rise for another 2 hours, until doubled in size.

15 Preheat the oven to 375°F (190°C). Brush the top of the dough with egg wash.

16 Bake in the middle of the oven for 40–45 minutes. If it's browning fast, cover with foil.

17 The bottom will sound hollow when ready. Leave to cool for 5 minutes, then turn out.

18 Remove the parchment paper and cool completely on a wire rack before dusting with confectioner's sugar to serve. **STORE** The panettone will keep in an airtight container for 2 days.

Panettone variations

Chocolate and Hazelnut Panettone

This variation of the classic panettone is a surefire winner with any children and any leftovers make a particularly delicious Bread and Butter Pudding (see recipe below).

SERVES 8 | 30 MINS | 45–50 MINS | UP TO 4 WEEKS

Rising and proofing time
3 hrs

Special equipment
High-sided panettone mold or 8in (20cm) springform cake pan

Ingredients
3¼ cups bread flour, plus extra for dusting
¼ cup sugar
1½ tsp dried yeast
½ tsp salt
5 tbsp unsalted butter, melted
2 large eggs, at room temperature
½ cup milk
1 tsp pure vanilla extract
⅔ cup (3oz) hazelnuts, coarsely chopped
finely grated zest of 1 orange
vegetable oil, for greasing
½ cup (4oz) dark chocolate chips, or dark chocolate chunks, coarsely chopped
1 small egg, for glazing
confectioner's sugar, for dusting

Method

1 Combine the flour, sugar, yeast, and salt in a mixing bowl. Whisk together the butter, eggs, milk, and vanilla extract in a bowl.

2 Add the liquid to the dry ingredients and bring them together to make a soft, sticky dough. Knead for about 10 minutes by hand, until it forms a smooth, elastic dough.

3 Form the dough into a loose ball and stretch it out on a floured work surface. Scatter the hazelnuts and orange zest on top and knead the dough again until well incorporated. Form the dough into a loose ball and put it in a lightly oiled bowl.

4 Put the bowl inside a large plastic bag and leave it to rise in a warm place for up to 2 hours, until doubled. Meanwhile, line the mold with silicone paper or double thickness parchment paper. If using a springform pan, make a ring of paper that forms a collar around the sides of the pan, finishing higher than the edge of the pan by 2-4in (5-10cm).

5 When the dough has doubled in size, knock it back and stretch it out again as in step 3. Scatter the chocolate over the surface and bring together, lightly kneading it before shaping it into a round ball just big enough to fit into the mold. Put it into the mold, cover it, and leave it to rise for another 2 hours.

6 When ready to bake, preheat the oven to 375°F (190°C). Brush the top with beaten egg, then bake in the middle of the oven for 45–50 minutes, covering with parchment paper after 20 minutes to prevent the top from browning.

7 Let the panettone cool in the mold for a few minutes before turning out to cool on a wire rack. Remove the parchment paper. Dust with confectioner's sugar to serve.

STORE The panettone will keep in an airtight container for 2 days.

Panettone Bread and Butter Pudding

Any leftover panettone can be turned into this quick and easy dessert. Try introducing different flavors such as orange zest, chocolate, or dried cherries to the dish before baking.

SERVES 4–6 | 10 MINS | 30–40 MINS

Ingredients
4 tbsp unsalted butter, softened
9oz (250g) panettone
1½ cups half-and-half, or a mixture of half heavy cream and half milk
2 large eggs
¼ cup sugar
1 tsp pure vanilla extract

Method

1 Preheat the oven to 350°F (180°C). Use a little softened butter to grease a medium sized, shallow baking dish.

2 Slice the panettone into ½in (1cm) thick slices. Butter each slice and lay them, overlapping slightly, into the baking dish. Whisk together the half-and-half, or cream and milk, eggs, sugar, and vanilla extract. Pour the liquid over the panettone and then gently press down on top to make sure it has all been soaked in the liquid.

3 Bake in the center of the oven for 30–40 minutes until it is just set, golden brown, and puffed up. Serve warm.

ALSO TRY...
Festive Panettone Pudding Plain panettone can also be spread with a little marmalade and the cream enriched with 1–2 tbsp whiskey and a grating of orange zest and nutmeg.

Individual Stuffed Panettones

Try these as an alternative dessert at a Christmas meal.

SERVES
6

1 HOUR

30–35 MINS

Rising, proofing, and chilling time
3 hrs proofing and minimum 3 hrs chilling

Special equipment
6 x 8oz (225g) ramekins

Ingredients
butter, for greasing
1 x panettone dough, see page 166, steps 1–9
7oz (200g) mascarpone cheese
7oz (200g) crème fraîche
1 tbsp Kirsch or other fruit liqueur (optional)
12 glacé cherries, quartered
4 tbsp pistachio nuts, coarsely chopped
confectioner's sugar, for dusting

Method

1 Grease the ramekins, then line them with parchment paper. The paper should stand about 2in (5cm) taller than the ramekins.

2 Cut the panettone dough into six, and place 1 piece in each ramekin. Cover, and leave to rise for 1 hour, or until doubled in size. Preheat the oven to 375°F (190°C).

3 Bake for 30–35 minutes. The panettones will be golden-brown. Remove 1 from its ramekin and tap the base. It should sound hollow. If it doesn't, remove all the panettones from their ramekins, place on a baking sheet, and bake for 5 minutes. Place on a wire rack and leave to cool completely.

4 Cut a disk from the bottom of each panettone, leaving a rim of around ½in (1cm). Use a gentle sawing action to lever the disk of bread out in 1 piece. Set aside.

5 Cut along the insides of the rim nearly to the bottom of the upside down panettone. Cut all around, then use your fingers to pull and scrape as much of the interior out as possible, leaving an intact shell.

6 Put the extracted pieces into a mini food processor and reduce to fine bread crumbs.

In a bowl, cream together the mascarpone and crème fraîche with the liqueur, if using.

7 Mix in the panettone crumbs and beat well. Fold through the cherries and pistachios. Pile the mixture back into the panettone shells and replace the disk of panettone you had set aside.

8 Wrap and refrigerate for at least 3 hours or overnight before unwrapping and dusting with confectioner's sugar to serve.

PREPARE AHEAD These will keep overnight in the refrigerator.

BAKER'S TIP
Panettone is an Italian sweet bread traditionally baked for Christmas. Although the process is lengthy, the time taken is mostly for the bread to rise twice. It is not complicated to make, and gives a marvelously light result unlike a store-bought panettone.

Bara Brith

This sweet Welsh "speckled bread" is at its best eaten the same day it is made, ideally while still warm and spread with butter.

MAKES 2 LOAVES | **40 MINS** | **25–40 MINS** | **UP TO 8 WEEKS**

Rising and proofing time
3–4 hrs

Special equipment
2 x (9 x 5½in/23 x 13cm) loaf pans (optional)

Ingredients
1 (¼oz/10g) package yeast
1 cup warm milk
¼ cup sugar, plus 2 tbsp for sprinkling
1 small egg, plus a little more, beaten, for glazing
3¾ cups bread flour, plus extra for dusting
1 tsp salt
4 tbsp unsalted butter, softened and diced
1 tsp pumpkin pie spice
oil, for greasing
1½ cups (8oz) dried mixed fruit (raisins, golden raisins, and mixed citrus peel)

Method

1 Whisk the yeast into the milk with 1 teaspoon of the sugar, cover with a towel, and leave in a warm place for 10 minutes until the mixture froths. Beat in the egg.

2 By hand, or in an electric mixer with a whisk attachment, rub the flour, salt, and butter together until the mixture resembles fine bread crumbs. Stir in the pumpkin pie spice and remaining sugar.

3 Make a well in the center of the dry ingredients. Pour in the milk mixture and bring it together with your hands to form a sticky dough. Turn out on to a lightly floured work surface and knead for up to 10 minutes. (If using an electric mixer, change to a dough hook and knead for 5 minutes.)

4 You should now have a soft, pliable dough. It should be quite sticky, but if it is not balling up into a single piece of dough, add a little more flour, 1 tablespoon at a time.

5 Place the dough in a lightly oiled bowl and cover with plastic wrap. Leave it to rise in a warm place for 1½–2 hours until doubled in size. Turn out on to a lightly floured work surface and stretch it gently out to a sheet around ¾in (2cm) thick.

6 Scatter the dried fruit over the dough and bring it together from the sides into the middle to form a ball again. Knead lightly for a couple of minutes until the fruit is well incorporated into the dough.

7 Shape the dough into your desired shape, or halve and put into the loaf pans. Cover with plastic wrap and a clean kitchen towel and leave in a warm place to rise for another 1½–2 hours, until again doubled in size.

8 Meanwhile, preheat the oven to 375°F (190°C). Brush the bread with a little egg wash and sprinkle it with 1 tablespoon of sugar. Bake for 25–30 minutes for loaf pans, or 35–40 minutes for a large freeform loaf. Cover halfway through cooking time with foil if it browns too much.

9 The bread is done when it is golden brown and firm and the bottom is hollow when tapped. Leave to cool for a good 20 minutes before cutting, as it will continue to cook after being removed from the oven. Cutting too early causes the steam to escape and the loaf to harden.

STORE The bread will keep in an airtight container for 2 days (see Baker's Tip).

BAKER'S TIP

As with most breads, baking two loaves and freezing one of them makes good sense when there is lengthy rising. Leftover bread can be toasted for a couple of days after baking, or sliced and used in Bread and Butter Pudding (see page 168).

Cinnamon Rolls

If you prefer, leave the rolls to rise overnight in the fridge (after step 15) and bake in time for a breakfast treat.

MAKES 10–12 | **40 MINS** | **25–30 MINS** | **UP TO 4 WEEKS**

Rising and proofing time
3–4 hrs or overnight

Special equipment
12in (30cm) springform cake pan

Ingredients
½ cup milk
7 tbsp unsalted butter, plus extra for greasing
1 (¼oz/7.5g) package dried yeast
¼ cup sugar
4¼ cups flour, sifted, plus extra for dusting
1 tsp salt

1 large egg plus 2 large egg yolks, at room temperature
vegetable oil, for greasing

For the filling and glaze
2 tbsp cinnamon
½ cup light brown sugar
2 tbsp unsalted butter, melted
1 large egg, lightly beaten

1 In a pan, heat ½ cup water, the milk, and butter until just melted. Let it cool slightly.

2 When just warm, whisk in the yeast and a tablespoon of sugar. Cover for 10 minutes.

3 Place the flour, salt, and remaining sugar in a large bowl.

4 Make a well in center of the dry ingredients and pour in the warm milk mixture.

5 Whisk the eggs and egg yolks and add to the mixture. Combine to form a rough dough.

6 Place on a floured surface and knead for 10 minutes. Add extra flour if it's too sticky.

7 Put in an oiled bowl, cover with plastic, and keep in a wam place for 2 hours until well risen.

8 Prepare the filling by mixing 2 tablespoons of cinnamon with the brown sugar.

9 When the dough has risen, turn it onto a floured work surface, and gently knock it back.

SWEET BREADS

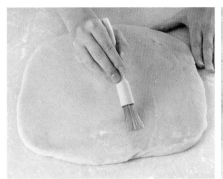

10 Roll it out into a rectangle about 16 x 12in (40 x 30cm). Brush with the melted butter.

11 Scatter with the cinnamon. Leave a ½in (1cm) border on one side and brush it with the egg.

12 Press the sugar mixture with the palm of your hand to ensure it sticks to the dough.

13 Roll the dough up, working toward the border. Do not roll too tightly.

14 Cut into 10–12 equal pieces with a serrated knife, being careful not to squash the roll.

15 Grease and line the pan. Pack in the rolls. Cover and let rise for 1–2 hours.

16 Preheat the oven to 350°F (180°C). Brush with egg and bake for 25–30 minutes.

17 Heat 3 tablespoons water and 2 of sugar until dissolved. Brush the glaze on the rolls.

18 Sprinkle with a mix of the remaining sugar and cinnamon before turning out to cool on a wire rack. **STORE** The rolls will keep in an airtight container for 2 days.

Sweet Roll variations

Chelsea Buns

These sweet and spicy buns were invented in the 18th century at The Bun House in Chelsea, London, where they proved a hit with royalty.

MAKES	30	30	UP TO 4
9	MINS	MINS	WEEKS

Rising and proofing time
2 hrs

Special equipment
9in (23cm) square cake pan

Ingredients
2¼ cups bread flour, sifted, plus extra for dusting
½ tsp salt
2 tbsp sugar
1 tsp dried yeast
3 tbsp butter, plus extra for greasing
1 large egg, lightly beaten
½ cup warm milk
vegetable oil, for greasing
1 cup (4oz) mixed dried fruit
⅓ cup light brown sugar
1 tsp pumpkin pie spice
honey, for glazing

Method

1 Mix the flour, salt, sugar, and yeast in a mixing bowl. Rub in 1 tablespoon of the butter. Pour in the egg, then the milk. Mix to form a soft dough. Knead for 5 minutes. Place in a lightly oiled bowl and cover with oiled plastic wrap. Leave in a warm place for 1 hour, or until doubled in size.

2 Grease the pan. Put the dough on a lightly floured surface and knead. Roll out to a 12 x 9in (30 x 23cm) rectangle. Melt the rest of the butter in a saucepan over low heat, then brush over the surface of the dough, leaving a border along the long edges.

3 Mix the fruit, brown sugar, and spice together and scatter over the butter. Roll up the dough from the long edge like a Swiss roll, sealing the end with a little water. Cut the dough into 9 pieces. Put the pieces in the pan and cover with plastic wrap. Leave to rise for 1 hour until doubled. Preheat the oven to 375°F (190°C). Bake for 30 minutes, then brush with honey and cool before transferring to a wire rack.

STORE The buns will keep in an airtight container for 2 days.

Spiced Fruit Buns

These delicious sweetened rolls make a perfect afternoon snack.

MAKES	30	15	UP TO 4
12	MINS	MINS	WEEKS

Rising and proofing time
1½ hrs

Ingredients
1 cup tepid milk
1 (¼oz/10g) package dried yeast
3¾ cups bread flour, sifted,
  plus extra for dusting
1 tsp pumpkin pie spice
½ tsp ground nutmeg
1 tsp salt
6 tbsp sugar
4 tbsp unsalted butter, diced,
  plus extra for greasing
vegetable oil, for greasing
1½ cups (6oz) mixed dried fruit
2 tbsp confectioner's sugar
¼ tsp pure vanilla extract

Method

1 Warm the milk until tepid, stir in the yeast, cover, and leave for 10 minutes until frothy. Place the flour, spices, salt, and sugar in a bowl. Rub in the butter. Add the yeasted milk to form a soft dough. Knead well for 10 minutes. Shape into a ball, then place in a lightly oiled bowl and cover loosely. Leave in a warm place for 1 hour until risen.

2 Place the dough onto a lightly floured work surface and knead in the dried fruit. Divide the dough into 12 pieces, roll into balls, and place, well spaced, on lightly greased baking sheets. Cover loosely and leave in a warm place for 30 minutes, until doubled. Preheat the oven to 400°F (200°C).

3 Bake for 15 minutes, or until the buns sound hollow when tapped on the base. Transfer to a wire rack to cool. While the buns are still hot, combine the confectioner's sugar, vanilla extract, and 1 tablespoon of cold water, and brush over the top of the buns to glaze.

STORE Keep in an airtight container for 2 days.

Hot Cross Buns

These sweet buns are too delicious to have just for Easter.

MAKES 10–12 | **30 MINS** | **15–20 MINS** | **UP TO 4 WEEKS**

Rising and proofing time
2–4 hrs

Special equipment
piping bag with thin nozzle

Ingredients
¾ cup milk
4 tbsp unsalted butter
1 tsp pure vanilla extract
1 (¼oz/10g) package dried yeast
½ cup sugar
3¾ cups bread flour, sifted,
  plus extra for dusting
1 tsp salt
2 tsp pumpkin pie spice
1 tsp ground cinnamon
1½ cups (6oz) mixed dried fruit (raisins, golden
  raisins, and mixed peel)
1 large egg, beaten, plus 1 extra for glazing
vegetable oil, for greasing

For the paste
1 tbsp all-purpose flour
1 tbsp sugar

Method

1 Heat the milk, butter, and vanilla in a pan until the butter is just melted. Cool until tepid. Whisk in the yeast and 1 tablespoon of sugar. Cover for 10 minutes until it froths.

2 Put the remaining sugar, flour, salt, and spices into a bowl. Mix in the egg. Add the milk mixture and form a dough. Knead for 10 minutes on a floured surface. Press the dough out into a rectangle, scatter over the dried fruit, and knead briefly to combine.

3 Place the dough in an oiled bowl, cover with plastic wrap, and leave in a warm place for 1–2 hours until doubled. Turn the dough out onto a floured surface, knock it back, and divide into 10–12 balls. Place them on lined baking sheets. Cover with plastic wrap and a kitchen towel and leave for 1–2 hours.

4 Preheat the oven to 425°F (220°C). Brush the buns with the beaten egg. For the paste,

mix the flour and sugar with water to make it spreadable. Put it into the piping bag and pipe crosses on the buns. Bake in the top of the oven for 15–20 minutes. Transfer to a wire rack and allow to cool for 15 minutes.

STORE The buns will keep in an airtight container for 2 days.

BAKER'S TIP
These traditional Easter buns are very different and far superior to their bland store-bought namesakes. They have a delicate, crispy exterior surface and a light, moist, fragrant crumb with authentically assertive levels of fruit and spice. They are delicious still warm from the oven, spread with plentiful cold butter.

Croissants

These may take some time to make, but the final result is well worth the effort. Start a day ahead.

MAKES 12 | **1 HOUR** | **15–20 MINS** | **4 WEEKS, UNBAKED**

Chilling time
5 hrs, plus overnight

Rising time
1 hr

Ingredients

2¼ cups plus 2 tbsp all-purpose
  flour, plus extra for dusting
½ tsp salt
2 tbsp sugar
1 (¼oz/10g) package dried yeast

1 cup milk, at room temperature
vegetable oil, for greasing
18 tbsp unsalted butter, chilled, cut
  into ½in (1cm) thick slices
1 large egg, beaten

1 Place the flour, salt, sugar, and yeast in a large bowl, and stir to blend well.

2 Using a butter knife, mix in enough warm water, a little at a time, to form a soft dough.

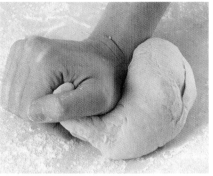

3 Knead on a lightly floured surface until it becomes elastic under your hands.

4 Place back in the bowl, cover with lightly oiled plastic wrap, and chill for 1 hour.

5 Roll the dough out into a rectangle that measures 10 x 17in (25 x 43cm).

6 Squash the chilled butter with a rolling pin, keeping the pat shape, until ½in (1cm) thick.

7 Place the butter in the center of the dough. Fold the dough over it. Chill for 1 hour.

8 Roll out the dough on a lightly floured surface to a 24 x 14in (61 x 36cm) rectangle.

9 Fold the right third to the center, then the left third over the top. Chill for 1 hour, until firm.

SWEET BREADS

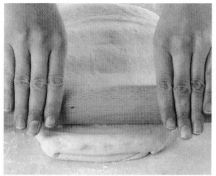

10 Repeat the rolling, folding, and chilling twice. Wrap in plastic wrap and chill overnight.

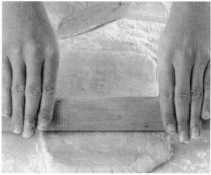

11 Cut the dough in half, and roll out one half to a 5 x 14½in (12 x 36cm) rectangle.

12 Cut into 1 x 5in (3 x 12cm) squares, then cut diagonally to make 6 triangles. Repeat.

13 Holding the ends of the longest side, roll it toward you. Curve into crescent shapes.

14 Place on baking sheets lined with parchment paper, leaving space between each.

15 Cover with lightly oiled plastic wrap. Leave for 1 hour until doubled in size. Remove the film.

16 Preheat the oven to 425°F (220°C). Brush them with egg, then bake for 10 minutes.

17 Reduce the temperature to 375°F (190°C) and bake for another 5–10 minutes.

STORE The croissants are best served when still warm, with butter and jam, but will keep in an airtight container for 2 days; gently reheat to serve.

Croissant variations

Pains au chocolat

Fresh pains au chocolat, still warm from the oven and oozing with melted chocolate, make the ultimate weekend breakfast treat.

| MAKES 8 | 1 HOUR | 15–20 MINS | UP TO 4 WEEKS |

Chilling time
5 hrs, plus overnight

Rising time
1 hr

Ingredients
1 quantity croissant dough,
   see pages 176–177, steps 1–10
7oz (200g) dark chocolate
1 large egg, beaten

Method

1 Divide the dough into 4 equal pieces and roll each out into a rectangle, about 4 x 16in (10 x 40cm). Cut each piece in half, to give 8 rectangles approximately 4 x 8in (10 x 20cm).

2 Cut the chocolate into 16 even-sized pieces. If you buy two 4oz (115g) bars, they normally divide naturally into 8 pieces each. Mark each piece of pastry along the long edge at one-third and two-thirds.

3 Put a piece of chocolate at the one-third mark, and fold the short end of the dough over it to the two-thirds mark. Now place a second piece of chocolate on top of the folded edge at the two-thirds mark, brush the dough next to it with beaten egg, and fold the other side of the dough into the center, making a three-layered parcel with pieces of chocolate tucked in on either side. Seal all the edges together to prevent the chocolate from oozing out while cooking.

4 Line a baking sheet with parchment paper, place the pastries on it, cover, and leave to rise in a warm place for 1 hour, until puffed up and soft. Preheat the oven to 425°F (220°C). Brush the pastries with beaten egg and bake in the oven for 10 minutes, then reduce the oven temperature to 375°F (190°C). Bake for another 5–10 minutes, or until golden brown.

STORE These will keep in an airtight container for 1 day.

Cheese and Ham Croissants

Ham combined with tangy cheese is used here to great effect.

| MAKES 8 | 1 HOUR | 15–20 MINS | UP TO 4 WEEKS |

Chilling time
5 hrs, plus overnight

Rising time
1 hr

Ingredients
1 quantity croissant dough,
   see pages 176–177, steps 1–10
8 slices ham, prosciutto, or Spanish chorizo
8 slices cheese, such as Emmental
   or Jarlsberg
1 large egg, beaten

Method

1 Divide the dough into 4 equal pieces and roll each out into a rectangle, about 4 x 16in (10 x 40cm). Cut each piece in half, to get 8 rectangles about 4 x 8in (10 x 20cm).

2 Place a slice of ham or slices of chorizo on the middle of each croissant and fold one side over it. Place a slice of cheese on the folded over piece, brush with beaten egg, and fold the remaining side over it. Seal all the edges. Cover and place in a warm place for 1 hour or until spongy and soft. Preheat the oven to 425°F (220°C).

3 Brush the pastries with egg and bake for 10 minutes, then reduce the temperature to 375°F (190°C). Bake for another 5–10 minutes, or until golden brown.

STORE Keep in an airtight container for 1 day.

> **BAKER'S TIP**
> These pastries are endlessly adaptable and can be made with a variety of fillings. Ham and cheese is the most common, but try using a layer of smoked ham and a layer of overlapped chorizo, and sprinkling with smoked paprika, for a more piquant flavor.

Croissants aux amandes

These frangipane-stuffed pastries are light and delicious.

MAKES 12 | **1 HOUR** | **15–20 MINS** | **UP TO 4 WEEKS**

Chilling time
5 hrs, plus overnight

Rising time
1 hr

Ingredients
2 tbsp unsalted butter, softened
⅓ cup sugar
¾ cup (3oz) ground almonds
2–3 tbsp milk, if needed
1 quantity croissant dough,
 see pages 176–177, steps 1–10
1 large egg, beaten
½ cup (2oz) sliced almonds
confectioner's sugar, to serve

Method

1 For the almond paste, cream the butter and sugar, using an electric hand mixer. Mix in the almonds, adding milk if too thick.

2 Cut the dough into 2 and roll half out on a floured surface to a 5 x 14½in (12 x 36cm) rectangle. Cut into 3 x 5in (12cm) squares, then cut diagonally to make 6 triangles. Repeat with remaining dough.

3 Spread 1 tablespoon of the paste onto each triangle, leaving a ¾in (2cm) border along the 2 longest sides. Brush the borders with egg. Roll the croissant up carefully from the longest side toward the opposite point.

4 Line 2 baking sheets with parchment paper and put the croissants on them. Cover and put in a warm place for 1 hour, until soft and spongy. Preheat oven to 425°F (220°C).

5 Brush the croissants with egg. Sprinkle with sliced almonds. Bake for 10 minutes, then reduce the temperature to 375°F (190°C). Bake for 5–10 minutes, or until golden. Cool. Dust with confectioner's sugar to serve.

STORE Keep in an airtight container for 1 day.

Danish Pastries

Although these deliciously buttery pastries take time to prepare, the home-baked taste is incomparable.

MAKES 18 · **30 MINS** · **15–20 MINS** · **UP TO 4 WEEKS**

Chilling time
1 hr

Rising time
50 mins

Ingredients
²⁄₃ cup warm milk
2 tsp dried yeast
2 tbsp sugar
2 large eggs, plus 1 for glazing,
    at room temperature
3½ cups all-purpose flour, sifted,
    plus extra for dusting
½ tsp salt

vegetable oil, for greasing
18 tbsp chilled butter
¾ cup good-quality cherry,
    strawberry, or apricot jam
    or compote

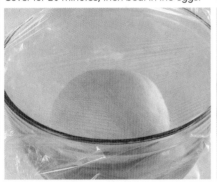

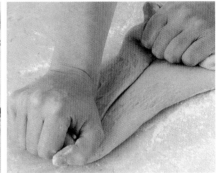

1 Mix the milk, yeast, and 1 tablespoon sugar. Cover for 20 minutes, then beat in the eggs.

2 Place the flour, salt, and remaining sugar in a bowl. Make a well and pour in the yeast mix.

3 Mix the ingredients into a soft dough. Knead for 15 minutes on a floured surface until soft.

4 Place the dough in a lightly oiled bowl, cover with plastic wrap and refrigerate for 15 minutes.

5 On a lightly floured surface, roll the dough out to a square, about 10 x 10in (25 x 25cm).

6 Cut the butter into 3–4 slices, each about 5 x 2½ x ½in (12 x 6 x 1cm).

7 Lay the butter slices on one half of the dough, leaving a border of ½–¾in (1–2cm).

8 Fold the other half of the dough over the top, pressing the edges with a rolling pin to seal.

9 Generously flour and roll it into a rectangle 3 times as long as it is wide, and ½in (1cm) thick.

10 Fold the top third down into the middle, then the bottom third back over it.

11 Wrap and chill for 15 minutes. Repeat steps 9–10 twice, chilling for 15 minutes each time.

12 Roll on a floured surface to ¼-½in (5mm–1cm) thick. Cut to 4 x 4in (10 x 10cm) squares.

13 With a sharp knife, make diagonal cuts from each corner to within ½in (1cm) of the center.

14 Put a teaspoon of jam in the center of each square and fold each corner into the center.

15 Spoon jam on the center, place on a lined baking sheet, and cover with a kitchen towel.

16 Keep for 30 minutes in a warm place until risen. Preheat the oven to 400°F (200°C).

17 Brush with egg wash and bake at the top of the oven for 15–20 minutes, until golden.

18 Leave to cool slighty then transfer to a wire rack. **STORE** These will keep in an airtight container for 2 days. **PREPARE AHEAD** Make up to end of step 11 and refrigerate overnight.

Danish Pastry variations

Almond Crescents

Butter, sugar, and ground almonds are combined here to make a delicious filling for these light and flaky, crescent-shaped Danish pastries. The pastry can be prepared the night before, ready for rolling.

| MAKES 18 | 30 MINS | 15–20 MINS | UP TO 4 WEEKS |

Chilling time
1 hr

Rising time
30 mins

Ingredients
1 quantity danish pastry dough,
  see pages 180–181, steps 1–11
1 large egg, beaten, for glazing
confectioner's sugar, to serve

For almond paste
2 tbsp unsalted butter, softened
⅓ cup sugar
¾ cup ground almonds

Method

1 Preheat the oven to 400°F (200°C). Roll half the dough out on a floured surface to a 12in (30cm) square. Trim the edges and cut out 9 x 4in (10cm) squares. Repeat with the remaining dough. Beat the butter and sugar until creamed, then beat in the ground almonds until smooth.

2 Divide the almond paste into 18 small balls. Roll them into sausage shapes a little shorter than the length of the squares. Place a roll of the almond paste at one edge of the square, leaving a gap of ¾in (2cm) between it and the edge. Press it down.

3 Brush the clear edge with egg and fold the pastry over the paste, pressing it down. Use a knife to make 4 cuts into the folded edge to within ½–¾in (1½–2cm) of the sealed edge.

Transfer to lined baking sheets, cover, and leave in a warm place for 30 minutes, or until puffed. Bend the edges in.

4 Brush with egg and bake in the top third of the oven for 15–20 minutes, until golden brown. Cool. Dust confectioner's sugar over to serve.

STORE The pastries will keep in an airtight container for 2 days.

BAKER'S TIP
Danish pastry recipes often call for the butter to be rolled out between pieces of parchment paper—or bashed with a rolling pin to render it pliable. This takes a lot of time. Use sliced chilled butter instead, for a fuss-free result.

SWEET BREADS

Cinnamon and Pecan Pinwheels

Try substituting hazelnuts or walnuts here if pecans are unavailable.

MAKES 16 | **30 MINS** | **15–20 MINS** | **UP TO 4 WEEKS**

Chilling time
1 hr

Rising time
50 mins

Ingredients
1 cup (4oz) pecan nuts, chopped
½ cup light brown sugar
2 tbsp cinnamon
1 quantity danish pastry dough,
 see pages 180–181, steps 1–11
1 large egg, beaten, for glazing
2 tbsp unsalted butter, melted

Method
1 To make the filling, mix the pecans, sugar, and cinnamon. Roll half the dough out on a floured work surface to an 8in (20cm) square. Trim the edges, brush the surface with half the butter, and scatter half the pecan mixture over the top, leaving a ½in (1cm) border at the long side that is farthest from you. Brush the border with a little egg.

2 Press the sugar mixture with the palm of your hand to ensure it sticks to the dough. Roll the dough up, starting with the long side and working toward the border. Turn seam-side down. Repeat.

3 Trim the ends and cut each into 8 slices. Turn over and press them to allow the edges to stick. Secure the ends of the dough with a cocktail stick. Line 4 baking sheets with parchment paper. Place 4 pastries on each sheet. Cover and leave in a warm place for 30 minutes, until well puffed up.

4 Preheat the oven to 400°F (200°C). Brush with egg and bake in the top third of oven for 15–20 minutes, until golden brown.

STORE The pastries will keep in an airtight container for 2 days.

Apricot Pastries

The pastry can be prepared the night before, so that 30 minutes of rising in the morning and a quick bake will give you fresh pastries in time for coffee.

MAKES 18 | **30 MINS** | **15–20 MINS** | **UP TO 4 WEEKS**

Chilling time
1 hr

Rising time
50 mins

Ingredients
1 quantity danish pastry dough,
 see pages 180–181, steps 1–11
½ cup apricot jam
2 x 14oz (400g) cans apricot halves

Method.
1 Roll half the dough out on a well floured work surface to a 12in (30cm) square. Trim the edges and cut out 9 x 4in (10cm) squares. Repeat with the remaining dough.

2 If the apricot jam has lumps, purée it until smooth. Take 1 tablespoon of jam and, using the back of the spoon, spread it all over a square, leaving a border of about ½in (1cm). Take 2 apricot halves and trim a little off their bottoms if too chunky. Place an apricot half in 2 opposite corners of the square.

3 Take the 2 corners without apricots and fold them into the middle. They should only partially cover the apricot halves. Repeat to fill all the pastries. Place on lined baking sheets, cover, and leave to rise in a warm place for 30 minutes until puffed up. Preheat the oven to 400°F (200°C).

4 Brush the pastries with egg and bake in the top third of the oven for 15–20 minutes, until golden. Melt the remaining jam and brush over the pastries, to glaze. Cool for 5 minutes then transfer to a wire rack to cool.

STORE The pastries will keep in an airtight container for 2 days.

Jam Doughnuts

Doughnuts are simple to make. These are light, airy, and taste far nicer than any store-bought varieties.

MAKES 12 | **30 MINS** | **5–10 MINS**

Rising and proofing time
3–4 hrs

Special equipment
oil thermometer
piping bag with thin nozzle

Ingredients
⅔ cup milk
5 tbsp unsalted butter
½ tsp pure vanilla extract
1 (¼oz/10g) package dried yeast
⅓ cup sugar

2 large eggs, beaten
2¼ cups all-purpose flour,
  plus extra for dusting
½ tsp salt
1 quart (1 liter) sunflower oil or
  vegetable oil, for deep-frying, plus
  extra for greasing

For the coating and filling
sugar, for dusting
¾ cup jam (raspberry, strawberry,
  or cherry), processed until smooth

1 Heat the milk, butter, and vanilla in a pan until the butter melts. Cool until tepid.

2 Whisk in yeast and 1 tablespoon of sugar. Cover and leave for 10 minutes. Mix in the eggs.

3 Sift the flour and salt into a large bowl. Stir in the remaining sugar.

4 Make a well in the flour and add the milk mixture. Bring together to form a rough dough.

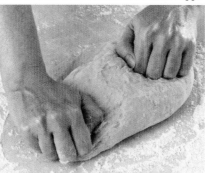

5 Turn the dough onto a floured surface and knead for 10 minutes until soft and pliable.

6 Put in an oiled bowl and cover with plastic wrap. Keep it warm until doubled; about 2 hours.

7 On a floured surface, knock back the dough and divide into 12 equal pieces.

8 Roll them between your palms to form balls. Place on baking sheets, spaced well apart.

9 Cover with plastic wrap and a towel. Leave in a warm place for 1–2 hours until doubled.

10 Heat a 4in (10cm) depth of oil to 340–350°F (170–180°C), keeping a lid nearby for safety.

11 Slide the doughnuts off the sheets. Do not worry if they are flatter on one side.

12 Carefully lower into the hot oil 3 at a time, rounded side down. Turn after 1 minute.

13 Remove with a slotted spoon when golden brown all over. Turn off the heat.

14 Drain on paper towels, then, while still hot, toss them in sugar. Cool before filling.

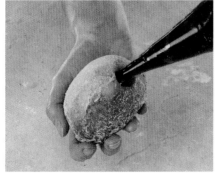

15 Put the jam in the piping bag. Pierce each doughnut on the side and insert the nozzle.

16 Gently squirt in about 1 tablespoon of jam, until it almost starts to spill out. Dust the hole with a little more sugar, and serve. **STORE** These will keep in an airtight container for 1 day.

Doughnut variations

Ring Doughnuts

Doughnuts are surprisingly easy to make, and home-cooked ones taste delicious. Don't waste the cut-out middles, just fry them separately for a bonus bite-sized treat.

MAKES 12 **35 MINS** **5–10 MINS**

Rising and proofing time
3–4 hrs

Special equipment
oil thermometer
1½in (4cm) round pastry cutter

Ingredients
1 quantity doughnut dough,
   see page 184, steps 1–6
1 quart (1 liter) sunflower oil or vegetable oil, for
   deep-frying, plus extra for greasing
sugar, for coating

Method

1 Turn the dough out onto a lightly floured work surface. Gently knock it back and divide into 12 balls.

2 Place the balls on baking sheets, spacing them well apart to allow room for spreading. Cover with plastic wrap and a paper towels, and leave in a warm place for about 1–2 hours until doubled in size.

3 Take a rolling pin and gently flatten the doughnuts to around 1¼in (3cm) in height. Oil the pastry cutter. Cut the centers out and set aside.

4 Pour the oil into a large saucepan to a depth of at least 4in (10cm) and heat it to 340–350°F (170–180°C). Keep the saucepan lid near and do not leave the hot oil unattended. Keep the temperature even, or the doughnuts will burn.

5 Slide the doughnuts off the baking sheets using a metal spatula. Don't worry if they are flat on one side; they will puff up on cooking. Add them, rounded-side down, into the hot oil and cook 3 at a time for about 1 minute, turning when the underside is golden brown. When golden brown all over, remove from the oil with a slotted spoon and drain them on paper towels. If you like, fry the cut-out centers in a similar way—these are very popular with younger children! Turn off the heat when finished frying.

6 While still hot, toss them in sugar and leave to cool a little before eating.

STORE These will keep in an airtight container for 1 day.

Custard Doughnuts

Custard is my favorite filling for doughnuts. Use good-quality, store-bought custard here—one that is made with real eggs and plenty of cream.

MAKES 12 **30 MINS** **5–10 MINS**

Rising and proofing time
3–4 hrs

Special equipment
oil thermometer
piping bag with thin metal nozzle

Ingredients
1 quantity doughnut dough,
   see page 184, steps 1–6
1 quart (1 liter) sunflower oil or vegetable oil, for
   deep-frying, plus extra for greasing
sugar, for dusting

For the coating and filling
sugar, for coating
1 cup ready-made custard

Method

1 Turn the dough out onto a lightly floured work surface. Gently knock it back and divide into 12 balls.

2 Place the balls on baking sheets, spacing them well apart to allow room for spreading. Cover lightly with plastic wrap and a paper towels, and leave in a warm place for 1–2 hours until almost doubled in size.

3 Pour the oil into a large, heavy-bottomed saucepan to a depth of at least 4in (10cm) and heat it to 340–350°F (170–180°C). Keep the saucepan lid nearby and never leave the hot oil unattended. Regulate the temperature, making sure it remains even, or the doughnuts will burn.

4 Slide the risen doughnuts off the baking sheets using a metal spatula. Do not worry if they are flatter on one side; they will puff up when cooking. Place them rounded-side down into the hot oil and cook 3 at a time for about 1 minute, turning as soon as the underside is golden brown. When golden brown on all sides, remove the doughnuts from the oil with a slotted spoon and drain them on paper towels. Turn off the heat when finished frying.

5 While hot, toss them in sugar and leave to cool. To fill the doughnuts, place the custard in the piping bag and pierce the doughnut on the side, where there is a perceptible mark, if possible. Make sure the nozzle goes into the center of the doughnut. Squirt 1 tablespoon of custard into the doughnut, until it almost starts to spill out. Dust the hole with sugar to disguise it. Serve.

STORE Keep in an airtight container for 1 day.

Churros

These cinnamon- and sugar-sprinkled Spanish snacks take minutes to make and will be devoured just as quickly. Try them dipped in hot chocolate.

SERVES **10** **5–10**
2–4 **MINS** **MINS**

Special equipment
oil thermometer
piping bag with ¾in (2cm) nozzle

Ingredients
2 tbsp unsalted butter
1½ cups all-purpose flour
¼ cup sugar
1 tsp baking powder
1 quart (1 liter) sunflower or vegetable oil, for frying
1 tsp cinnamon

Method
1 Measure ¾ cup boiling water into a bowl. Add the butter and stir until it melts. Sift together the flour, 2 tablespoons of the sugar, and the baking powder into a bowl.

2 Make a well in the center of the flour mixture and slowly pour in the hot butter mixture, beating, until you have a thick paste (you may not need all the liquid). Leave the mixture to cool and rest for 5 minutes.

3 Pour the oil into a large, heavy-bottomed saucepan to a depth of at least 4in (10cm) and heat it to 340–350°F (170–180°C). Keep the saucepan lid nearby and never leave the hot oil unattended. Regulate the temperature, making sure it remains even, or the churros will burn.

4 Place the cooled mixture into the piping bag. Pipe scant 3in (7cm) lengths of the dough into the hot oil, using a pair of scissors to snip off the ends. Do not crowd the pan, or the temperature of the oil will go down. Cook the churros for 1–2 minutes on each side, turning them when they are golden brown.

5 When done, remove from the oil with a slotted spoon and drain on paper towels. Turn off the heat when finished frying.

6 Mix the remaining sugar and the cinnamon together on a plate and toss the churros in the mixture while still hot. Leave to cool for 5–10 minutes before serving while still warm.

STORE These will keep in an airtight container for 1 day.

BAKER'S TIP

Churros are an almost instant treat, and can be made in only a few minutes. The batter can be enriched with egg yolk, butter, or milk, but the basic quantities of liquid to dry ingredients should be maintained. The thinner the batter, the lighter the results, but frying with a liquid batter takes a little practice.

Index

Page numbers in **bold** indicate step-by-step illustrations of recipes or techniques. Page numbers in *italics* indicate Baker's Tips.

About the author

After spending years as an international model, Caroline Bretherton dedicated herself to her passion for food, founding her company, Manna Food, in 1996.

Her fresh, light, and stylish cooking soon developed a stylish following to match, with a catering clientele that included celebrities, art galleries, theaters, and fashion magazines, as well as cutting edge businesses. She later expanded the company to include an all-day eatery called Manna Café on Portobello Road, in the heart of London's Notting Hill.

A move into the media has seen her working consistently in television over the years, guesting on and presenting a wide range of food programs.

More recently Caroline has worked increasingly in print, becoming a regular contributor to *The Times on Saturday*, and writing her first book, *The Kitchen Garden Cookbook*.

In her spare time, Caroline tends her beloved allotment near her home in London, growing a variety of fruits, vegetables, and herbs. When she can, she indulges her passion for wild food foraging, both in the city and the country.

She is married to Luke, an academic, and has two boys, Gabriel and Isaac, who were more than happy to test the recipes for this book.

Acknowledgments

The author would like to thank
Mary-Clare, Dawn, and Alastair at Dorling Kindersley for their help and encouragement with this massive task, as well as Borra Garson and all at Deborah McKenna for all their work on my behalf. Lastly I would like to thank all my family and friends for their tremendous encouragement and appetites!

Dorling Kindersley would like to thank
The following people for their work on the photoshoot:

Art Directors
Nicky Collings, Miranda Harvey, Luis Peral, Lisa Pettibone

Props Stylist
Wei Tang

Food Stylists
Kate Blinman, Lauren Owen, Denise Smart

Home Economist Assistant
Emily Jonzen

Baking equipment used in the step-by-step photography kindly donated by Lakeland. For all your baking needs contact: www.lakeland.co.uk.

Caroline de Souza for art direction and setting the style of the presentation stills photography.

Dorothy Kikon for editorial assistance and Anamica Roy for design assistance.

Jane Ellis for proofreading and Susan Bosanko for indexing.

Thanks to the following people for their work on the US edition:

Consultant
Kate Curnes

Americanizers
Nichole Morford and Jenny Siklós

Thanks also to Steve Crozier for retouching.